CAMP DAVID

PRESIDENTS

THEIR FAMILIES AND THE WORLD

JACK BEHRENS

AuthorHouse™ LLC
1663 Liberty Drive
Bloomington, IN 47403
www.authorhouse.com
Phone: 1-800-839-8640

Published by AuthorHouse   05/16/2014

ISBN: 978-1-4918-9858-1 (sc)
ISBN: 978-1-4918-9856-7 (hc)
ISBN: 978-1-4918-9857-4 (e)

Library of Congress Control Number: 2014908422

For information visit: www.writerjackweb.com
Graphics and production were prepared by Lisi Design, Holland Patent, NY.

TABLE OF CONTENTS

Photo Credits

To John
with lots
of great memories
Jack

ACKNOWLEDGEMENTS

Associate Editors: My wife Gert Behrens who was my
inspiration to finish this task which I began 54 years ago
and Kathleen Randall, New Hartford, NY

Principal Sources: Helen and Bill King, Camp David;
Congressmen Donald Mitchell and
Sherwood Boehlert, New York

Editor: Ken Arnold, Utica, NY

Graphics, cover, layout: *Lisi Design*, Holland Patent, NY
Beth Spoon, Rhonda Lisi, Stephen Lisi

Promotion, News Releases: Bill Randall, New Hartford, NY

INTRODUCTION & COMMENTARY

When the Lord Talks, People Listen. I did.

It was stranger than fiction. I've been tested before as my wife and immediate family know. But I've never experienced what happened that night (Wednesday, Dec. 11,2013) and like previous encounters I won't forget the softness of His voice, the sudden stillness as I listened to my- self breathe and the straight forward message I received. Then there was his quiet composure as He took me from the depths of my own despair to soaring with the kind of optimism every author should have as he reaches the last stages of his work. It more than made up for months of stagnation on paragraphs and rewrite and rewrite after rewrite.

The ordeal was over. The manuscript was done.

But let me back up a minute. This is no ordinary story. The people are very ordinary yet very exceptional Americans.

The idea for this book about the presidential retreat sprang from my mind after seeing a photo in a Sunday Parade Magazine of Soviet Premier Nikita Khrushev and US President Dwight Eisenhower smiling at each other at a place called Camp David, Maryland. I had been to Maryland a number of times but I didn't remember ever seeing a fort or army base named Camp David. I started this search 35 years ago. My Cleveland Browns had mauled the Los Angeles Rams for the NFL championship.. Secretary of State John Foster Dulles warned us that the ability to get to the brink is" getting to the verge without getting into war" No, you won't find any maps with directions. Nor will you today.

The government has removed all such reminders as well as directional signs and consequently, I've spent the last 35 years, gathering information about a place that exists but doesn't exist. Even Forest Rangers working in nearby Cunningham State Park won't give you an answer. The federal government releases little information about the camp to protect the president, his family and their guests. Understandable to a degree but when you consider hundreds of millions of tax payer dollars now being spent to house and protect   one family who may or may not be in residence at any time it does cause alarm. A law enforcement officer I know said it's the price we bear for being the only beacon for freedom (and that is flickering erratically) in a world turned upside down with predators and Halloween characters with guns. It seems to get worse with each holiday.

I realized later when I talked with a forest ranger that for my purposes and anyone else on the ground in Frederick County, MD Camp David doesn't exist. It's a secret site which means the public is not welcome. Deception is what governments do but are we deceiving ourselves by showing citizens we practice exactly what our enemies do? We seem to fail to succeed at spying. Thus, most Americans dismiss our efforts and remain skeptical of our results. Yet, we persevere, relying on America ingenuity to bring us a home run with bases loaded.

I became concerned about Camp David when I gave an oral survey about the subject in two of my upper level classes at Utica College. One class of 14 students had no idea what it is or where it was. In the other class only one student out of 19 knew it was a military base. The rest had no knowledge it was in Maryland or what it represented. When tax money is being spent for such secrecy... all of us have to worry including the military.

To assure myself that everyday folks know something of this side of America that we haven't voted for or individually approved I asked five intelligent and conscientious citizens their opinions of such shadowy issues. Here's what they think about Camp David:

Deborah Herrmann, a teacher in Oneida County, NY: teacher with an interest in American history, believes that maintaining Camp David at the cost discussed is "unconscionable" in today's world though she recognizes what the site meant in history. "My familiarity with Camp David is primarily with the Camp David Accord the president with his immediate family and for government matters." she said. "I think Camp David could be an ideal hiding place during an emergency but it would have to remain private and secret." Camp David needs to be "available on call" for use. It would probably require additional security. Should Camp David no longer be used, then it could become a national museum or sold to reduce the huge national debt.

Ben Benson, historian, collector of historical documents, signatures, New Hartford, NY: Ben has spent over 50 years collecting presidential documents and signatures and believes authenticity is most important in everything surrounding the subject. "For example, Roosevelt wanted a place where he could not only escape the heat and humidity of Washington but have an escape from reporters and the hectic pace of the White House. He usually relaxed on his boat where he loved to sail and the sea surrounding him. However, to be practical and conduct every day affairs, it was decided to seek a country retreat not too far from DC. He found such a place, a military camp that was soon to be converted to a federal retreat. Once established in 1935 he christened it 'Shangri-La'. This while reading James Hilton's book Lost Horizon. Here he could be practical and conduct everyday business.

The concept of an escape from the glare and hectic activity came from Lincoln, certainly many administrations ago. Lincoln sought refuge from a White House that was open to the public at large. He and his family enjoyed the tranquility of the Soldiers and Sailors Home outside Washington. Grover Cleveland owned a rustic cabin where they could escape from the onslaught of the media. Lou Hoover, President Hoover's wife who convinced him to purchase property in the Raritan area of Virginia mostly where he fished. Before leaving office he bequeathed his property to the government. When FDR took office his aides thought this fishing camp of the Hoovers' was a bridge too far. I believe anything connected to Hoover, FDR would veto because of his intense dislike of the man. An old camp, not that far from the White House, was purchased as a retreat for the president and his family. Opinions vary on the future of Camp David. Many say the retreat should be open to the media and the public as is the White House. FDR liked Spartan furnishings and the existing camp with old furniture. The president didn't like the fishbowl atmosphere of the White House. Shortly afterward, he renamed territory "Shangri-La" and that name would remain until President Dwight Eisenhower renamed it in honor of his grandson, David.

> *FDR liked Spartan furnishings and the existing camp with old furniture. The president didn't like the fishbowl atmosphere of the White House. Shortly afterward, he renamed territory "Shangri-La" and that name would remain until President Dwight Eisenhower renamed it in honor of his grandson, David.*

He believes history plays a part in the decision. "I believe we should keep the original name that FDR gave it because of its mystique and that Franklin Roosevelt is rated the top of our greatest presidents. The name Shangri-La invokes a place of distinction that Camp David cannot match. It inspires while the name David is more meaningful of the everyday. The camp is a presidential retreat and should be remembered as such."

Jerry Freeze Owner of the Cozy Restaurant, Inn and Museum offered his views by reminding people that those who serve in elected positions give up privacy. A president and his/her family have to learn to adapt their lives to a public that frequently doesn't care. Other elected officials face similar hardships and whether we share their political positions or not we need to recognize their time and service. Says Jerry: "If the men at the top in this country

Camp David Presidents 11

can't have a retreat where they can go to rest and not worry about interruptions I think we're not giving the president what he needs. I think the president deserves his privacy.

Dr. John "Jack" Heisse, teacher, medical practitioner, Burlington, Vt. is no longer with us but he pointed out the president is there so infrequently, the area could be opened for tours a day or two a week in selected parts of the camp. This could be done by the National Parks Service. "On further reflection, I have changed my mind. I now believe the public should be excluded from Camp David. It should be kept strictly for the use of the president. It should be for his private relaxation and entertainment. Should Camp David be used to entertain foreign diplomats? "That's a bad idea," he responded. "I've attended a few of those parties and I didn't see the purpose of those affairs then and I don't see them now. I don't see using Camp David for parties for the rich and famous. In some instances that's already happened. That denigrates the place and takes away from the purpose at the same time. I don't know why parties became more important than the outcome of important meetings. That's what democracy is, sharing views."

The management of the camp is also an area of concern to Dr. Heisse. "I feel it should be for the use of the president and should be carried as an item of the national budget. How this can be done I am not certain but certainly oversight is necessary to remove the suspicion of subterfuge and doubt that currently exists. It certainly shouldn't continue as an unbudgeted item. It needs greater management not less."

Should Camp David, an area acquired under duress by the federal government as the US entered war in 1942, sell the rights or ownership? "I do not believe it should be sold," Jack responded.

"This was a temporary arrangement as I understood the terms. The president didn't have the right to buy a part of a state in any event. Furthermore, there should be no name change from Camp David back to Shangri-La. We should stick with what we've got not muddy what has already been done. To change the décor there should be a limit to the ambiance and character of the entity, he said. "This should be budgeted in the overall budget that maintains Camp David."

And what of the future? "It is what it is," Jack Heisse noted. "We wouldn't change Lincoln's bedroom would we? What was done in 1942 in an emergency should be retained as heritage to be respected."

"Should First Ladies be allowed to change the décor? It is my feeling to a limited degree they should be allowed to change the décor keeping it with a rustic ambiance."

These folks expressed the surprise and disgust that you may feel when you read how thirteen presidents and their families discuss their thoughts about living a "good life." I certainly don't blame any president for reaching for a benefit offered. I do believe all of them could reach into their hearts and souls and find they could give back much of what they've taken. To start such a goodwill effort I'm making sure that 20 percent of the proceeds of this book, after costs, go to the people who really count, wounded veterans of America's wars. We all owe it to ourselves to help in whatever we can. This is my small contribution.

by John "Jack" Behrens

FRANKLIN D. ROOSEVELT

1933 · ROOSEVELT · 1945

Chapter 1

How A CCC Camp in Maryland Became Roosevelt's Hideaway

If Franklin D. Roosevelt would have had his way, he would have been cruising the waters around Washington DC in his yacht, the Potomac, even after World War II started. He didn't necessarily see himself as a target of the axis powers. His aides were increasingly concerned that he didn't recognize the danger. They worried about his safety and his non-chalance.

In March, 1942, security people around the president told the National Park Service to find a land site "reasonably close to the Washington area for use as a presidential retreat." The Navy was also very alert to the danger that the Potomac could no longer traverse even in the gentle coastal waters where US shore lights were visible. The threat of German U-boats was very real. There was speculation that German admirals were very aware of FDR's movements within the United States and coastal passage ways. The Chronicle of 20th Century reported US ships were being attacked on both coasts and the country didn't have enough warships to patrol the miles of open water. In September, 1941, a German sub damaged the USS Green off Iceland. Later the same month, the USS Kearney lost 11 seamen when it survived a torpedo explosion and, days later, on a bloody Halloween, U-boats attacked and sank the battleship USS Reuben James, leaving 76 dead or missing. Just a few months later, Americans in Santa Barbara, CA, saw the coming war up close and personal when a Japanese sub surfaced and attacked the coastal city and shelled a nearby oil refinery.

Intercepts told both Germany and Japan that American munitions stockpile was low and its military capability was marginally adequate.

At the same time, Roosevelt aides were realizing the commander in chief was noticeably weaker and showing the strain of endless meetings and mobilization planning. The pressure of potential world conflict was affecting FDR. His doctors worried about the coming summer months in oppressive Washington heat and humidity. Could an exhausted president suffering from paralysis and other serious illnesses handle the decision making? Consequently, the Park Service established criteria for making a land site available for a presidential retreat including elevation requirements to ensure coolness, as well as, careful plans for security.

Roosevelt was reluctant to give up his yacht, the Potomac, because of delightful memories of day cruises, evening cocktails, and leisurely conversation with an entourage of guests and his love of the water. The Potomac was the 6th vessel designated by the government for presidential use. It was a refurbished patrol boat used by the tiny US Coast Guard at the time.

It was turned into a "floating White House" to permit the president to get the relief and rest he needed to relieve his sinus and asthma. There was another plus, too. He loved to fish and the boat allowed him the luxury of taking a weekend to return to his favorite fishing holes along the coast. To put it in service, ship's carpenters and mechanics built a small bunk cabin with an adjoining bathroom and sleeping basket for his constant companion Fala. The ship also had a saloon with a large table for dinner parties and a presidential bathtub that FDR designed himself. While certainly not luxurious to yacht owners today, it was very functional for a handicapped president and his pet. To get to either deck, an electric pulley was installed to serve as an elevator in a false smokestack to lift Roosevelt and permit him to get around the yacht. Roosevelt, however, preferred to use a rope pulley. He felt he needed the exercise to strengthen his upper body.

The selection of Civilian Conservation Corps Camp #3 was created by the Park Service in cooperation with the president and his staff. The CCC, which came from the president's New Deal

team, has reminders of its work throughout the US with stadiums, public libraries, public schools and municipal buildings still standing and in use. The camp was one of three the team examined in an accelerated search along the east coast relatively close to the capital. The choices quickly narrowed to; Furnace Mountain on the Virginia side of the Potomac River below Harper's Ferry; the Shenandoah National Park, VA and the Catoctin Recreational Demonstration Area near Thurmont, MD. The final site was actually one of two camps; #3 and #4. Number four was later dropped because it hadn't been developed beyond cutting roads into the rugged terrain. Hi-Catoctin, as Camp #3 was first called, was to be a camp for federal government agents and their families by the WPA in 1935. It opened in 1938 originally to be used by federal government agents and their families under the guidance of the WPA. In 1942 President Roosevelt converted it to a retreat.

The use of a CCC camp and WPA workers were other bonuses for the government. The work force didn't just clear the land and do unskilled work, but was a talented group of craftsmen. They built virtually everything at Shangri-La. Shop workers fashioned ironware and hinges for gates, doors, lighting fixtures, tables and window frames. Dams and lakes were considered impractical so workers built concrete swimming pools with modern recirculation plants to use water from nearby streams.

Said Anne Cissel in her interesting book, Thurmont Scrapbook, the mountain was considered a recreational treasure. "In 1954, about half of the approximately 10,000 acres was transferred to and became Cunningham Falls State Park. The remaining acreage .Three (camps) ---Misty Mount, Greentop, and Camp Hi-Catoctin---were built; but construction never began on the fourth. One of the camps, Hi-Catoctin was to serve the families of federal employees, but became the private retreat of the President of the United States and closed to the public. Camp Round Meadow was built by and for the WPA as a base camp. It was later used as a group camp. Buildings were added in the '60s by the Job Corps. In the '70s, the camp became a seasonal folk culture center."

Roosevelt had sought to acquire the land at one time but he told a press conference later: "There's a place up there not far from Frederick (MD) that belongs to a man who doesn't like me; he's going to give it to the government someday, but he didn't want the president going there."

The Shenandoah plot was about 100 miles from the nation's capital and 3,000 feet above sea level. Some staffers liked its location because they were familiar with the park. As you drive through you can see its beauty. On the other hand, it was a longer

drive to Washington at the time. Probably the most damaging evidence against the Shenandoah was that, to provide adequate quarters, the cost was expected to run over $150,000, something the president didn't want to ask Congress for in a time of war. It would have taken a minimum of three months, once a decision was made, to begin.

But someone in the bowels of the Roosevelt Administration, it appears, had already made a calculated decision on the location. Two days before the park surveyors were to visit the Catoctin Mountains, the White House Communications Agency (WHCA) was already setting up equipment at Chestnut Lodge at Camp #3. Both #3 and #4 were approximately 70 miles from Washington but while camp #4 was in the initial stage, camp #3 already had rough buildings in place and some lines laid. A good portion of the land had been cleared. The CCC never built the 4th camp.

Security experts were already impressed with the Catoctin choice. There was natural foliage for both land and aerial camouflage. The natural wood buildings were all but invisible from the air because of the dense forest

surrounding the camp. A low flying plane would have great difficulty seeing much among the trees, a security official said.

"The highway, which ran to the entrance, was a prohibited thoroughfare with limited access. A ten foot barbed wire overhang encircled the compound. Sentry booths were provided at regularly spaced intervals and each booth was equipped with a telephone for general alarm if necessary. Flood lights around the perimeter were controlled by a single switch as was a second set of lights around the president's lodge, "said the Guided Tour of Camp David website available in the early days of the 21st century, but taken down as mysteriously as it went up. Secret Service gave the site a thorough review. They learned the names of neighbors, tested the soundness of the camp buildings, walked back and forth on mountain roads and in the surrounding woods. Physically, they said, Shangri-La was ideally situated at the peak of the mountain. Years later, there are only memories of the log cabin and a sailor on sentry duty by two gleaming anchors on each side of the gravel road.

Equally important, the Park Service thought the site could be readied within a short time for less than $25,000 by altering some buildings. Roosevelt, mindful of a possible Republican and Democratic outcry at such spending, personally scrutinized the Shangri-La cost reducing it to about $16,800.

How do you furnish such a government retreat? Like many Americans who have family cottages for summer months, furniture in the attic or basement is a starting point. Used White House and other federal building office surplus became the rummage sale that provided the retreat with its needs. The "Bear's Den,"

 for example, had a weathered old conference table which was placed under a rustic and discolored wheel chandelier and both made their way to the retreat in the Catoctin Mountain.

Personal hygiene was always difficult at Shangri-La. Shortly after workers completed the 20 duplexes, they were put in service, most without running water. Washing facilities for most who worked at the camp until more than a year after the war started, consisted of outside metal troughs with cold water only and some without any cover.

President Roosevelt called it his "Shangri-La," but for security reasons, it wasn't explained or identified to the media until much later. Early press conference transcripts showed that reporters didn't pursue the matter either. "Shangri-La was a beautiful, mythical mountain enclave where people had found the elixir of longer life and were trying to live it," one reporter said, suggesting it appeared as a setting in the Himalayan Mountains in Tibet. It fascinated FDR. It came from popular novelist James Hilton's book, Lost Horizon, which the president was reading at the time. Within days of briefly mentioning the place, Roosevelt told reporters that an air attack on Tokyo military targets and the heart of the Japanese government had been launched from an American aircraft carrier, Hornet, in a raid with a code name Shangri-La by a brave group of US air crews led by Col. Jimmy Doolittle. While even the most optimistic thought it was a doomed mission, it did rally the American public which suffered pain and disappointment as losses of airmen and land troops climbed in the thousands early in 1942.

Actually, the president was mindful of the "day of infamy" inflicted by Japanese forces and followed up with a meeting of the Joint Chiefs of Staff at the White House on Dec. 21, just two weeks after Pearl Harbor. He believed mainland Japan had to be attacked. The problem was the American military had few weapons of destruction, or planes to deliver them, that could reach Japanese soil and return let alone damage it.

The Air Force used 16 modified B-25B Mitchell medium bombers and launched them from the deck of the Hornet deep in the western Pacific Ocean. The purpose of the mission was to cast doubt on Japan's arrogant attitude of invincibility following its successes and the progress made in capturing allied ports and cities on the Pacific Ocean as it gathered momentum needed to wage and win the war. The raid came just nine days after the US announced it had lost 36,000 dead and wounded or missing defenders in the battles for Bataan and the Philippine Islands.

Said most reports after the American air strike, the raid suc-

ceeded in its goal of helping American morale and casting doubt in Japan on the ability of the Japanese military leaders. It also caused Japan to withdraw its powerful aircraft carrier force from the Indian Ocean to defend their home islands . . ." It did minor damage and little to harm the Japanese war effort but it revitalized the United States and recommitted its people to longer work hours and higher productivity in producing war material.

All American aircraft were lost and 11 crew members of the original 71 officers and 130 enlisted airmen and army maintenance personnel selected and trained for the mission, were either killed or captured, three of them seized in China and  executed. More exasperating to the allies, Russia, which was considered an ally, confiscated one of the bombers that landed in Vladivostok and the crew was interned for more than a year. Media remembered that Roosevelt was jaunty and confident at the press conference that followed the raid. When asked the details and where US bombers had come from, Roosevelt removed the filtered cigarette from his lips, smiled and said: "Shangri-La ." He knew that confidence was crucial at this point. He had no confirmation of the results of the raid.

Roosevelt spent that April visit to the site planning his retreat. Said his son Eliot later about Hi-Catoctin: . . ."it looked more like a Marine training camp made up of rough pine cabins, but it suited father down to the ground---metal beds, bathroom door that refused to shut , bare walls ornamented with some of his favorite cartoons." He penciled an estimate of how he wanted the main lodge arranged and a note to accompany the sketch: "Fix up one cottage for Miss Hackmeister and the stenog; fix up one cottage for Mr. Hassett and the other male staff; fix up one cottage for Filipinos and valet---6 bunks." After looking at the site work, he chose an existing cabin with an open porch and an outside kitchen and huge fireplace then he gave specifications for a hinged

wall that could be used as an emergency exit ramp to accommodate his handicap. An underground intercommunications system that eventually connected water, power and telephone lines was underway almost immediately. A long first day ended at 5:55 p.m. when the caravan returned through Frederick and the familiar trip to the White House with the president ready for his evening martini and a cigarette. Work started in May and was nearly completed in June when the USS Potomac crew was transferred to Hi-Catoctin. He gave the lodge (later called Aspen) the appropriate name The Bear's Den.

Except for the Bear's Den, most latrines were outhouses. Imagine signing on to work in the woods and find no indoor plumbing! Entertainment besides reading and taking long walks in a beautiful forested region where you had to remember to follow signs on the trees to remain on the path and return to your lodging. Marines and Secret Service patrolled the compound after the president's arrival. They used war dogs which created the fear of being challenged and the panic of forgetting the password for the day. Going to the bathroom in the dark and being confronted by a dog and his handler could change your mind about your need to visit the latrine!

Some suggest Roosevelt missed his calling; he could have been a gag writer or an ad copy writer. While it's unknown who did the artwork, cartoon figures began showing up with all kinds of labels for different cabins. Since FDR had to approve it or allow it to be displayed, it offers a look at the president's sense of humor in the midst of orchestrated chaos. Here's a sampling of the work:" 221 B Baker Street" for the Secret Service, "The Roost" for the guests,

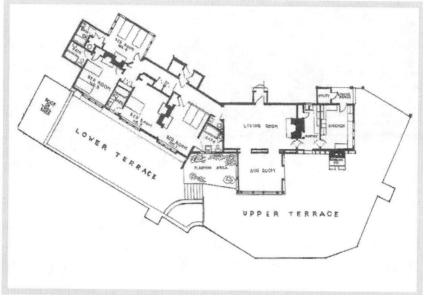

Drawing Courtesy of *The President is At Camp David* by Dale Nelson (SU Press)

the "Bread Basket" for the mess hall, the president's physical therapist, Lt. Commander George Fox, was housed in a cabin called "The Pill Box:" the various drinking fountains were known as "Water Holes," the bath house was called "The Hickory Limb," the laundry was named "Soap Dish;" the swimming pool was titled "Bear Wallow" and the communications cabin was named "One Moment Please." The main entrance gate was labeled "Tell it to the Marines." However, one of the lodge names showed another side of the president; "Little Luzon" where the Philipino stewards were housed. But, then, it was a different era and civil rights issues hadn't been tested.

Marines who handled security were quartered at Camp Misty Mount just a few miles from the retreat. More than 100 Marines, commanded by a Col. Brooks, patrolled the president's compound. Brooks had been in charge of the detachment at Warm Springs, GA, when the president visited the resort. The Marines shared the duty with the Secret Service.

When Shangri-La was completed, it had about 20 duplex cabins and several miscellaneous buildings. Some of these structures were used to house guests, regular camp crew and others. According to early records, there may have been as many as a hundred people on board with the president; his doctor, a medical assistant, cryptographers, radio operators, telephone operators, chauffeurs, valet, projectionists and Secret Service in that first few months.

Original staff members had to be flexible and multi-talented because of all the tasks that evolved from starting a camp. Buildings and roads were developed and had to be maintained, fences were constantly mended, land still had to be cleared, grounds had to be policed, retaining walls built and water and fire departments were established.

One morning with a Secret Service agent at the wheel, FDR had his driver turned the vehicle into a private road running through a large estate. The two men arrived at the caretaker's cottage where they were confronted by a small woman carrying a large shotgun, who demanded to know who they were. She absolutely refused to believe their responses and when they admitted they did not have the owner's permission to be there, she raised the shotgun in a threatening manner and pointed it at them.

Roosevelt was given all the protection a president should have but he did have a knack for getting himself in trouble with his political enemies. He never visited Thurmont but he did like to take rides in the beautiful Maryland countryside which unfortunately, was sprinkled with homes and summer places of Republican business leaders firmly against his policies. One morning with a Secret

Service agent at the wheel, FDR had his driver turn the vehicle into a private road running through a large estate. The two men arrived at the caretaker's cottage where they were confronted by a small woman carrying a large shotgun, who demanded to know who they were. She absolutely refused to believe their responses and when they admitted they did not have the owner's permission to be there, she raised the shotgun in a threatening manner and pointed it at them. They made a most difficult U-turn on that narrow road with the shotgun still pointed at them and departed quickly. The next morning, property owner, Charles Paine, was called to the White House by Secret Service agents and told what had happened. He was taken to see the president and, after apologizing, wrote him a letter and sent a permit along to assist him in using the road. No one knows if the permit was ever used.

The president's security detail also had the responsibility for keeping the location of the Maryland retreat from a curious me-

dia. Security personnel did an effective job for several years while there was tight security on the president's travel and location. Rumors in the nation's capital had Roosevelt visiting former President Herbert Hoover's old camp on the Rapidan in the Shenandoah National Park, one of the spots the president's staff examined during the search for a retreat. The White House rumor was fueled by staff members who felt the wider it was circulated, the better the ruse. It was a Washington society writer, Evelyn Peyton, who infuriated FDR and the White House by revealing the actual location. Roosevelt wasn't worried about security so much as he was concerned that his own staff would allow his favorite retreat---Shangri-La ---to be placed off limits from that time forward. To keep the lid on the story when the United Press International wire service released an article saying the president's summer house was in "the rolling Catoctin Mountains of Western Maryland,"

 the National Park Service confirmed the fact that the president had, in fact, used the location on several occasions. They referred all questions to the National Capitol Park Service which sent them on routinely to the White House never to be answered!

The issue came up again weeks later when the war in Europe ended and the Pacific war was in the final days. Meanwhile, reporter Frank Henry of the Baltimore Sun, along with photographer, Frank Miller, rented a plane and flew over the retreat taking photos. The photographer and Henry did try talking to Secret Service before they flew their mission but Secret Service agents were reluctant to discuss the site because of secrecy. The government agency changed its position once photos were published in the Sun's Sept. 16, 1945 issue. But, the agency still refused to let the two newsmen into the compound.

Thirteen days later, however, reporters and photographers from major news organizations were informally invited to tour Shangri-La and get the first inside view of the grounds and much of the interior. It was a historic event, considering the secrecy that shrouded the mountain for three years. But, there was no follow up to discuss permitting media continued access to the retreat.

Said an untitled document prepared by those familiar with the history of the early days of the retreat: "Although every effort was taken to ensure the secrecy of the place, residents of Thurmont knew its location. They even had an infallible method of knowing when the president was coming. Before all presidential visits, a Marine sentry would stand guard at the little bridge that crossed Big Hunting Creek on the road up to the mountain. Although the residents of Thurmont knew the day, they did not always know the hour. Usually the presidential party would drive through Frederick and the word would be relayed via telephone. His party would skirt Frederick and then he'd more than likely take us by surprise."

What was it like with the president at Shangri-La? Dale Nelson's excellent account, The President Is at Camp David, gives a detailed description. But, Harry Hopkins, a special assistant to the president, was almost always "on board with FDR at the camp," said many of those I interviewed. The two men would spend considerable time reviewing cables and reports and Hopkins would put together replies with the president's help. Good weather (a luxury not routine for Maryland in the mountain) would find them on the screened porch or outside on the patio. Windy weather would move them into the living /dining room. They were accompanied by FDR's longtime secretary, Grace Tully. Her assistant, Dorothy Brady, usually was along to do all the dictation and typing.

The untitled document gives us a look at the routine of the president's life when he began journeying to the retreat: "Our cars finally rolled out of the south grounds (of the White House) at 3:55 (pm) and having taken a circuitous route, reached Shangri-La at 6:05 (pm). The president settled himself on the porch to the rear of his cottage; said we would have dinner at 7 and cocktails in 10 minutes. The president was as good as his word; (he) lost no time in shaking martinis on the porch. After dinner the president went back to his favorite corner of the porch and asked for his stamps, always a diversion." It rarely varied. Something else that rarely changed was the remainder of the day. The president would usually retire early just after walking to Captain Jack Keeves cabin for a brief visit.. Keeves was the US Navy officer in charge at Shangri-La.

The term "retreat" was certainly better than "hideaway," but for members of the US public, it was still a hideaway. Citizens were told the president had such a place and that it was private not open to the public.

While Shangri-La was a retreat from the pressure of formalities and the daily challenge of answering staff and visitors' questions and attending meetings, the purpose of the camp was to permit the president of the United States to dress informally, chat with selected colleagues, friends and visiting statesmen, as well as relax with family.

The term "retreat" was certainly better than "hideaway," but for members of the US public, it was still a hideaway. Citizens were told the president had such a place and that it was private not open to the public. What wasn't told to the American people, and continues as mystery today, was that it has been taxpayer funded for more than 70 years.

Camp David was and is a place for casualness and informality as you will learn in this look at America's once isolated gathering place committed to keeping the country safe. Slacks and athletic clothing have been the custom since the beginning. There never was any formal routine and, except for the Bush wedding, the dress code was casual. In the early days, the president liked to sit on the screened-porch talking, working on his stamp collection, playing solitaire, catnapping or doing whatever amused him. If he was reading or working on his stamps or meditating, no one intruded. There was never such a thing as an unscheduled caller.

He had a telephone in his bedroom directly connected to the White House on which he could make out-going calls, but anyone calling him went through the Camp David switchboard operator.

As a government official once stated, this secluded little mountain retreat not only had the data on the fighting fronts and the potential fighting fronts but was actively in touch with them all.

When an important call came to the camp switchboard he was notified. He would go to his phone and tell the White House to connect him. That continued to change with Dwight Eisenhower and those who followed him, as technology caught up with the folks on the mountain.

Life for those who worked at the Shangri-La, that became Camp David, came in spasms, I was told. "Although a retreat, Shangri-La was a place where much work was accomplished." It served as more than a retreat for President Roosevelt. As a government official once stated, this secluded little mountain retreat not only had the data on the fighting fronts and the potential fighting fronts but was actively in touch with them all. For example, Roosevelt was at Shangri-La when he received news "by direct radio communication" that American forces had landed at Algiers establishing a second front. On Prime Minister Winston Churchill's first visit to the Catoctin Retreat, the two received word of the king of Italy's resignation. It was at Shangri-La that the president received the news of the allied landings at Sicily and the resignation of Mussolini." It proved to be unfounded, as Roosevelt wrote in his log; rumor proved false much to our regret.' That same afternoon, President Roosevelt sent a cable to Prime Minister Churchill which said: "When the news from Rome came this afternoon, by coincidence I was at Shangri-La again. This time it seems to be true." The cable went on to discuss the terms for surrender and the course of the war to follow.

While the war consumed chunks of time daily, President Roosevelt's work load at Shangri-La was as diverse as his presidential duties. Here's a snippet from presidential assistant William D. Hassett for August 1942 as FDR and staff members tried to rebuild American confidence after several months of dismal news from the war fronts:

"The day was one of important conferences for the president. He is working on three important speeches: one to be delivered Monday afternoon at the dedication of Medical Center in Bethesda; another to the youth of the world from the White House Thursday noon and third, and most important of all, outlining the president's plan to control inflation will be delivered from Hyde Park. All of this deals with, perhaps, the most important phase of the war since Pearl Harbor.

"On Saturday morning, Averell Harriman arrived to discuss his conference in Moscow with Winston Churchill and Joseph Stalin. He shared the cabin called "The Roost" with Mr. Hassett.

Later that afternoon, General Arnold and a Dutch general arrived for conferences with the president. On Sunday, Aug. 30, the president decided to return to Washington after lunch. When, after an afternoon of fog and drizzle, the sun appeared at 5 p.m. and the party departed Shangri-La for Washington."

FDR realized the value of face to face meetings in comfortable surroundings and away from the sounds of war. Long before Jimmy Carter, Richard Nixon, Bill Clinton, Ronald Reagan or the two Bushes, he saw the value of an American countryside as an ideal way to bring about settlements and compromises and "selling" an American attitude with belligerent, as well as, friendly leaders. The president began the practice of inviting foreign heads of state to the wooded Catoctin Mountain site. "During the war, Prime Minister Winston Churchill made two visits to the site. On May 11, 1943, he accompanied Mr. Roosevelt to Shangri-La for a three-day weekend. The two returned the following weekend. As the two drove through Thurmont, their motorcade stopped at an intersection. As the Secret Service agents stood on the cars, people

in the vicinity rushed to see the two heads of state. The crowd cheered and Prime Minister Churchill made his famous Victory sign as the motorcade continued up the mountain."

Churchill enjoyed the interplay and exchanges with average citizens that came on the final two visits. The Prime Minister and the president explored the western part of Maryland and made a visit to Thurmont's night life stopping by for an ice cream cone at Jerry Freeze's Cozy Restaurant and talking to customers. Churchill got into the swing of things when he gave a waitress some coins and played the juke-box. Nobody remembers the numbers he selected, but it could easily have been Glenn Miller's String of Pearls or Moonlight Serenade, both high on the Hit Parade list at the time. Miller spent time in England preparing his military orchestra to join the invasion forces and play for the allied troops. He was declared missing in action (later dead) when the light plane he had hitched a ride on went down in the English Channel as the invasion of Normandy, France began.

Churchill and Roosevelt both enjoyed fishing and during the construction of the Catoctin Recreation Development Area, trout streams were much improved thanks to a nudge from the president and the efforts of wildlife experts in the US government. Roosevelt told a number of visitors it was one of the reasons he wanted the Catoctin selected for the camp site. And, he went out of his way to ensure his fishing excursions were successful. While he had little success with the streams at the point where Little Hunting Creek emptied into an ore pit of the old Catoctin Iron Furnace, he hit paydirt where it became a wider and deeper pond; he struck a fisherman's gold. The Park Service made sure that the pond was stocked with plenty of brook trout and when the agency knew of the president's plans to visit it, would restock the water hole. The president would be driven to the pit and then a sailor or Marine would take him in a rowboat where he would relax, cast for trout and tell others about his catches.

When motion pictures became available and wartime hits were shown at the White House they helped the White House staff and the president understand the violence and destruction of war. Wartime movies were shown in the White House in a place called "the family theater" and featured 20th Century News reel footage along with other documentary films.

The first film ever shown at 16 Pennsylvania Avenue was during President Woodrow Wilson's tenure; it was the controversial D.W Griffith's film, The Birth of a Nation, described as "a history written with lightning." The White House Theater was constructed the first year of the war so that the president could see Signal Corps and Hollywood footage of the combat on all fronts. Obviously, other Hollywood entertainment was also shown to guests of the period. A White House cloak room offered an idea of the size of the room which later became the White House Family Theater.

They were expected earlier but the transition from Roosevelt to Truman was made difficult because FDR had shared so little with the new president. Truman, for example, didn't know about the atomic bomb nor did he officially know of the existence of Shangri-La.

Several months later, the sewer line at Witch Hazel backed up." We thought we had repaired that when we repaired the line at the president's lodge," King said. "At first, I thought it might just be clogged. After a while it became clear that the back hoe used on the first job had taken out part of the drain pipe and we had not replaced it when we filled the trench. Such things happen regardless of who and where you are," he added.

The Trumans didn't show up at Shangri-La until September, 1945. They were expected earlier but the transition from Roosevelt to Truman was made difficult because FDR had shared so little with the new president. Truman, for example, didn't know about the atomic bomb nor did he officially know of the existence of Shangri-La. The retreat was actually deserted after the president's death except for a 20 person maintenance crew that did necessary work at the 125-acre site during the summer months. Rumors became the spin of the time. One was that the camp was being prepared for the new president. Another was that the administration was looking into the sale of the place. A third was that other government agencies might use it. President Truman and his wife Bess visited Shangri-La in mid-September and they gave camp personnel the impression they were "interested" in preserving the Roosevelt era retreat but they weren't enthusiastic about it for themselves. The Trumans made several other trips up the mountain that fall and on each of those visits, Harry told Lieutenant Commander William Rigdon, assistant naval aide to the president and officer in charge at Shangri-La, that he felt "cooped up because of the trees and underbrush which grew up right along the wall of the

Main Lodge." He told Rigdon he wanted it removed. The president said that he "might feel better about the place if the growth were thinned out. The commander in chief's wishes became an order and a working party from the presidential yacht USS Williamsburg reported to duty at Shangri-La to take on the task. "With axes, saws and bulldozers they cut down trees, rooted out stumps and cleared the underbrush. After blisters, strained muscles and sore backs, there appeared a wide open lawn on the east side of the lodge that sloped down to the forest and flagstone fence," said the untitled document on the effort. Concern came the same day from the security people who could see too much of the thinning could bring bad results. A compromise was reached and the work was finished.

The changes set the stage for President and Mrs. Truman to make their first official visit to the camp. That, unfortunately, came on a rainy day in late fall. Mrs. Truman found the place, "dull and uninteresting." President Truman, said those near him, almost immediately lost interest in returning and talks of selling the place resumed. But, Bess had a change of heart.

On Mother's Day, 1946, Harry and Bess were joined by mother-in-law, Mrs. David Wallace, to have lunch at the wooded retreat, as it displayed spring colors in leaves and foliage that were impressive. The change of heart about the Maryland camp seemed to come from the president, but it did reflect Mrs. Truman's thoughts, too.

The trip to the retreat was very different this time. On previous journeys, it was clearly seen as a government caravan with flashing lights on the front and back of vehicles. It always appeared to other motorists as an attempt to clear the way for more important people.

Not this time. The cars were plain sedans with District of Columbia licenses, not official Washington, DC, plates. Meantime, the Secret Service "relaxed" wartime procedures and they remained in their cars at a discrete distance behind the president. Truman actually drove his family to the retreat. Agents didn't surround the car at traffic stops in Frederick, either.

The president used Shangri-La as his own gym; he loved to walk. He usually did so accompanied by the camp commander, Lieutenant Commander Rigdon. According to the Secret Service, these were the only times the president was out of their sight. The service and the president had a number of disagreements over his whereabouts when at the retreat. They wanted him to stay on the main roads. "The president favored a myriad of trails and he refused to back down from that position," aides said. "He also

38 *by John "Jack" Behrens*

enjoyed roaming the camp. With Mrs. Truman at his side and the Secret Service in the backseat along with OIC Rigdon, the president, irritated the security detail assigned to him," presidential observers reported.

Mrs. Truman, at particular times of the year, discovered what many had told her: the Catoctins are beautiful in the fall, can be in the spring and certainly are in the summer.

President Truman took an additional step which wasn't announced, but it was accepted as policy; he opened the camp to members of his staff when he and Bess were not in residence.

She decided to bring her Garden Club to Shangri-La for luncheons which sometimes including a poolside buffet. The ladies enjoyed it and suddenly the Truman's were taking another look at the presidential retreat.

Heat was a serious concern and forced modifications because it had been built purely for warm weather, although some cottages did have fireplaces. Consequently, President Roosevelt closed the camp each winter. Truman, who could see a use for the retreat now that Bess enjoyed it, decided to keep it open and all buildings were made secure and tight for winter use. More fireplaces were added and steam heat was installed in the main lodge and some of the guest cabins.

President Truman took an additional step which wasn't announced, but it was accepted as policy; he opened the camp to members of his staff when he and Bess were not in residence. When the policy changes were instituted, Shangri-La became used part of nearly every week and always on weekends. Though records are hard to find, many of the Truman Administration and other White House staffers benefitted from the change. Social life at Shangri-La continued to improve as more people found it a "good duty station."

There were restrictions on the use of facilities on the base, however. First, only a select group were authorized the privilege and then only when the visit would not interfere with the use by the president and his family. It was also understood that if it was a visitor, not an official guest of the president, he or she would pay for their meals and other expenses incurred.

Guests were expected to comply with camp regulations required for security and operational reasons. While there were no clothing restrictions, there was a zero tolerance for bizarre behavior, wild parties and inappropriate language. Excessive drinking and gambling for high stakes were totally prohibited.

During the Truman Administration, unlike the Roosevelt years, Shangri-La was considered a place for relaxation. Wartime security and tension created the stress of duty from April, 1942, until the fall of 1945. With air raid sirens silent, blackouts lifted and people walking or bicycle riding, Truman would take his family and sometimes other guests to the movies at the Navy Mess on the base. The president usually took mile and a half walks with Lieutenant Commander Higdon and he noted work done within the camp. Friends said the President thought it was his duty to make sure the base was always ready for inspection. Observers said his eyes were always scanning the buildings, sidewalks and roadways, and he usually had a cogent comment about something that needed more attention. When the weather was bad,

Truman would remain in the Main Lodge, otherwise the walk would be followed by a swim or sunbathing.

The Trumans took few guests to Shangri-La, the number was far less than Roosevelt, who thrived on having people around. On a number of occasions, the Trumans went alone to the retreat. Other times, Commander Higdon was the only staff member to accompany them. On occasion, the President went by himself, when Mrs. Truman wasn't in Washington.

Roosevelt thoroughly enjoyed card games to challenge himself. Some think it was the reason Shangri-La was important to him. Excessive drinking and gambling were not permitted, but the two presidents both were card players. Roosevelt could use cards to outwit those who thought his happy exterior was how he played the game.

And, he certainly enjoyed a small bet every so often. Truman, by contrast, was a poker player from his early days in Missouri politics and the army. The president made it clear there would be "no wild parties" at the camp but that people were free to use the facilities as long as they followed the regulations. He was against any gambling but he also occasionally placed small bets.

As Harry Truman's presidency ended, the cloak of secrecy that had veiled the mountaintop quietly was pulled back, but the media still wasn't permitted inside the compound. The explanation was that there were security risks that caused the government to

not let reporters or broad-
casters and cameras into
Shangri-La. Jerry Freeze's
Cozy Restaurant again
played a role in assisting reporters and newscasters on
assignment. They would
travel to Thurmont and get
a room for several days.

Some would double up to keep the costs down for media organizations, as well as, freelancers. Once a day, a camp representative
would travel to Thurmont to brief reporters on the story of the
day...or what if anything happened at the Main Lodge.

The Freeze family had a long and pleasant relationship with the
occupants of the White House, whether Democrats or Republican.
From the time government officials began arriving at Thurmont
and work started at Hi-Catoctin, they shared mutual interests.

The wartime restrictions virtually vanished and the Marine
detachment at Camp Greentop left and security became an internal matter. All staff members were given a camp memorandum
which explained the dos and don'ts of their tenure at the retreat
and told not to divulge the contents to anyone.

In 1951, the situation changed again. The North Koreans attacked the South Koreans and major war loomed once more.

Bibliography

Camp David Tour (home.mchsi.com/~cbretvet?/Tour/CD04/.html

Doolittle Raid (http://en.wikpedia.org/w/index.php?title=Doolittle_Raid&printable=yes)

www.writerjackweb.com

Kessler. Ronald, Inside The White House, Random House, 1995

Welcome Aboard, Camp David Tour website Camp David Presidential Retreat, www.fas.org/nuke/guide/usa/c3i/campdavid.htm

Camp David, http://en.wikipedia.org/w/index.php?title=Camp_David&printable=yes Catoctin Mountain Park chapter 6, War and Politics Shape the Park, circa 1950s

Shangri-La: Where WWII Decisions Were Made, Jack Behrens' www:writerjackweb.com. October,2007

HARRY TRUMAN

1945 · TRUMAN · 1953

Chapter 2

Give 'em Hell Harry

The sudden death of Franklin D. Roosevelt, April 12, 1945, as the war in Europe was ending and the Pacific war grew more intense was a shock to many because the American people didn't really know how sick the president was. No one could have been more in the dark than the vice president, Harry S. Truman.

The battle in the Pacific became Harry Truman's war.

He also discovered the truth about the rumors in Washington; a massive bomb being built to end the war but he wasn't privy to details. More insulting perhaps was that Roosevelt had a top secret hideaway where he and his cronies met to play cards and talk. Harry had never been invited! Even more revealing were the discussions about how the defeated countries were to be carved up after the war. Again, Truman was ignored. "I have decided because of the historical events of national interest now associated

It was six months later that Truman, his wife Bess and his daughter Margaret made their first journey to Shangri-La on a rainy September day.

with the Catoctin Recreational Area that this property should be retained by the federal government and made a part of the Department of Interior. This action is in accord with the position expressed by the late President Roosevelt before his death." He was loyal to the party and the man who chose him to a national ticket regardless of the slights and insults. He had not been raised that way, he told close friends and associates. Harry was the product of a middle class family who couldn't afford college. He was hoping to matriculate to West Point after high school in 1901 and become an officer in the United States Army. He was versatile; he had worked in different enterprises. He had held jobs in farming, oil drilling, and banking. But he failed the eye exam and had to return home.

Bess and Harry Truman

It was months later that Truman, his wife Bess and his daughter Margaret made their first journey to Shangri-La on a rainy September day. He told the officer in charge, Lt Commander William M. Rigdon, his assistant naval aide, he felt too cooped up with all the underbrush that had grown up all around the camp. A work party from the yacht USS Williamsburg, went to work cutting down trees, removing stumps and clearing the foliage.

Later, the Trumans told friends the place was boring and needed more work inside and out. He told friends he really didn't want to spend time in such a place. While he told the crew they did a great job he confided in others about the use of the place and how much improvement it needed.

Nearly a year later, Mother's Day, 1946, the president decided to have lunch at Shangri-La with his wife and mother-in-law, Mrs. David Wallace. While the official government didn't indicate how the Trumans felt about the camp, they didn't volunteer their thoughts either. Bill Safire, a former Nixon speechwriter, in his book Before the Fall, said FDR, while born to wealth "appreciated rusticity; Nixon, born poor, appreciated a heated swimming pool right out front." The trip (to Shangri-La) initiated a change in travel to the mountain retreat. Roosevelt had traveled to the Catoctins in an official motorcade each time. Truman, by contrast, journeyed to the camp in a plain sedan licensed in the District of Columbia. The Secret Service, while it had concern about the change and the president's safety, followed a short distance behind his car. Wartime security had been relaxed and, consequently, when the president's car came to a red light in Frederick, MD, agents didn't rush to surround the vehicle as they had done with Roosevelt. They remained in their cars. Truman had already made the decision to upgrade the camp and use it.

Staff and guests including Mrs. Roosevelt and the Truman family weren't enthusiastic about accompanying the president to the retreat in the days just after the war. "Arrangements were simply to the point of crudeness. . .His cottage had only two baths, one of them his. The other was shared by three bedrooms and the president laughingly alerted his guests to the fact that the bathroom door did not close securely. Presidential aides roomed in crude pine cabins scattered about the area," said historian James M Burns in his book Roosevelt: The Soldier of Freedom.

During the Roosevelt years, for example, the camp was closed during the winter months. But Truman decided the camp could be used during the winter months and so steam heat was installed in the Main Lodge and some of the guest cabins.

But like all expansion plans snags happen. When his daughter Margaret's piano forced the floor under it to sag and it was ruled unsafe, changes had to be made. Some plans were cancelled and others put on hold. When an inspection found rotted timber not only in one section but others of the building, projects were cancelled because the cost escalated. The Trumans moved across the street to the Blair House Camp David was shelved as the Executive Mansion became the focus of reconstruction. The entire interior of the building was removed in a project that took more than three years.

The new president also decided he wanted the retreat used by members of his staff when he and Bess weren't at the site. It was a policy change never addressed by the Roosevelt Administration. Thus, Shangri-La became a place for weekly social events.

The new president also decided he wanted the retreat used by members of his staff when he and Bess weren't at the site. It was a policy change never addressed by the Roosevelt Administration. Thus, Shangri-La became a place for weekly social events. However, within a few months, he changed his mind about staff use of the facility. Only a select few within his cabinet were given special permission to use the still secret Maryland hideaway.

While the official government narrative about Camp David claimed the Trumans rarely used the retreat, they were known by camp regulars to have visited and enjoyed the beautiful countryside and facilities on occasion. Harry occupied himself hiking the trails that virtually surrounded the retreat.

Bess continued to complain that there was lack of things to do at Aspen Lodge while Harry spent long hours wandering the mountainside with a Secret Service man who was forced to become a hiker whether he wanted to or not. Secret Service details assigned to Truman  found the president set a brisk pace. It was also noted that as the retreat became more user friendly to Bess she reciprocated. For example, she had her ladies' groups visit the White House during the summer months and held various events outdoors. President Truman never shied away from controversy even after he left the White House. In 1962, he told several newspapermen with typical Truman wry humor that his middle name didn't stand for a name it was a compromise between two families and grandfathers about how Harry would be addressed. The grandfathers, Anderson Shipp Truman and Solomon Young, found it acceptable and it became the approved version after 1962. The Truman Library reported that in the 1960s the use of Harry's name became a controversy especially among editors. However editors found that Truman's own use of a period "after the S is very obvious."

Furthermore he neglected to let others know who recorded his trips to Key West in official log books but didn't follow the same procedure when traveling to Frederick, MD. Some believe that he regarded trips to Key West as souvenirs for family and staff. For example, the president never mentions whether House staff and military personnel joined him at Key West. It is assumed that some meetings with staff were classified because of the tensions of the times. It was noted later that Harry became the 33rd president of the United States less than three months after taking the office of vice president. The new president had joined the military in 1917 like millions of other men and served until 1919 when he left the military service as a captain. Over the course of late 1940s to the early 1950s the president faced some of the most complex problems a world leader could face.

In 1947, The Trumans received an unsolicited Christmas gift, a beautiful blond Cocker Spaniel. Bess and Harry decided not to keep the dog and gave it to the White House physician, Brig General Wallace Graham. The Trumans caught the wrath of dog lovers throughout the country and the president was branded "anti-canine." Dr. Graham, who grew tired of the constant complaints after he had the dog for a short time offered the cocker named Feller, to Truman's naval aide Admiral James K. Foskett to "end" or "bury" the story. The admiral left Feller with Quartermaster Chief George Poplin. The dog actually had three more owners before it was given to a Greenfield, OH farmer who kept Feller until he died of old age. The Truman family offered a slightly different view of their brief adoption of Feller. In January, 1948, Margaret said the family had to give up the dog because Margaret would not be around to raise Feller because Bess did not wish to raise the puppy herself. The Trumans similar to others wanted to be pet-free. Not an easy thing to do

when there are children in the house and neighborhood. It was noted in a later web site that Margaret received a gift of an Irish Setter while she was living in the White House. "Mike" the Setter stayed on White House grounds for a short while.

"The Bear's Wallow"

FDR's swimming hole so appropriately named for bodies floating past actually survived three later presidencies. It was also used by Truman, Kennedy and Johnson. Later, Navy personnel used it on occasion as new facilities were added.

What was it like to work at the camp? Listen to John James, a native of Chicago, then a young Marine bugler. He had just arrived from a ceremonial detachment in Washington. He had never lived in a rustic cabin with a potbellied stove for heat let alone camped out in the woods. "At the time, the president's secret mountain camp. . . in the Catoctin Mountains sounded great. Besides, I'd had my fill of ceremonial duty at the White House. It was interesting, but not why I'd joined the Marines," he said in a magazine article later. "The hideaway was reached via a long, winding gravel road that climbed to the top of the mountain. I shared a cabin with 10 to 12 other Marines and our heat came from a potbellied stove. Before any presidential visits, we were required to practice our security measures. Our first dry run, guards marched a platoon through the woods, dropping off a Marine at each. At my hut, I was told to check out the communications equipment then wait until everyone else reached their assigned posts. But when I opened the door, there were at least five Copperhead snakes on the floor! Slamming the door shut, I ran after my platoon for help. No one seemed too surprised when the Marine assigned 'snake duty' was called they were removed. Just in time, too," he said. The President and his family arrived shortly afterward.

Meanwhile, the US government launched its "Salvage for Victory" to collect the needed tin, rubber, scrap iron and rags and paper for the war effort. Within a period of days in April, a Japanese assault throughout the Philippines captured some 70,000 allied troops. It was the beginning of the murderous Bataan Death March which claimed nearly 10,000 lives and saw some 12,000 become prisoners of the Japanese and marched 85 miles.

What did bother Harry Truman about the job of being president? "I do not know of any easy way to be president. It is more than a fulltime job and the relaxations are few. I used to take the

presidential yacht as well as the Little White House less for holidays than to hideaway and they were useful when I wanted to catch up on my work and also when I wanted to consult with my staff without interruptions."

It was a hell on earth for the emaciated survivors of General Douglas MacArthur's Pacific command.

By mid-May the first issue of the military newspaper that rallied the troops Stars and Stripes was published.

Loyal to the core Harry S. Truman didn't confide his hurt or anger to anyone but his wife Bess. Yet it was Harry Truman who, when discussions of the disposition of Shangri-La, said that he believed that it should be retained for posterity. "I have decided that it should remain as it is," he told an aide.

DWIGHT D. EISENHOWER

1953 — EISENHOWER — 1962

Chapter 3

The World's Hero

Dwight and Mamie Eisenhower brought a level of "home owner-ship" when the Allied Supreme Commander became US president and a resident of both the White House and Camp David.

Camp David wasn't a showplace when the Eisenhowers arrived. By being a secret location and opened occasionally it was a musty collection of old furniture and odds 'n' ends from government attics when it opened in 1942.

The Catoctin Mountain retreat was the least of Ike's concerns. He and Mamie were restoring their farm near Gettysburg close by, he was involved with world affairs, the aftermath of World War II and finding ways to cut costs in federal spending while ending a war called the "Korean Conflict." Like his predecessor Harry Truman, he was a man of simple tastes and had few interests beside golf. He enjoyed a strong drink and a hamburger.

Mamie, of course, had far more grand plans for the camp after the shock of her first visit wore off. She probably was as turned off at what she saw as Bess Truman. She made it clear that things would have to change before she would return. Eventually they did, thanks to her influence on her husband and her strong personality. Before the dust had settled, Ike, at Mamie's urging, was renaming camp buildings. Mamie noted that the indigenous plants on the mountaintop told a story too. She proposed and the camp director accepted the proposition that lodges would be named for trees in the area. That was later revised to include

---

Mamie noted that the indigenous plants on the mountaintop told a story too. She proposed and the camp director accepted the proposition that lodges would be named for trees in the area. That was later revised to include plants as well.

---

plants as well. Mrs. Eisenhower introduced a tree from her native state of Colorado---the Aspen---and gave it to the president's residence. The president's lodge is still called Aspen. Mamie thought, and the president agreed, that names like Witch Hazel, Birch, Maple, Dogwood, Red Oak, Poplar, Cedar, Chestnut, and Hickory---the names of trees on the mountaintop---were more interesting and less self-serving than the "Bear's Den," "Little Luzon"_ and other colorful titles from the Roosevelt era. There was one excep-

tion: former camp administrator Bill King's wife Helen was asked to name one of the last cabins and she chose the flower Rosebud. Smaller buildings at the camp were torn down to provide more space. "Mamie came to like the camp in time," said King. "Although their farm was close by they still visited Camp David as often as possible. Most often they would join the guests and sit and play cards and watch movies. Ike would walk out in the yard and hit a golf ball or two and then go to the skeet range. Before the range was put in, I remember, he shot skeet from the patio."

Things were changing. In the final year of the Truman Administration, the Congress and state governments passed the 22nd Amendment to the Constitution which limited the president to only two terms. Roosevelt's unprecedented four terms and death on eighty-third day of his eighth year at 63 caused concern and trauma as the public became more aware of how sick Roosevelt was as he struggled to lead a country at war and deal with world leadership. They may have been among the reasons Harry Truman withdrew his name in the presidential race and Sen. Adlai Stevenson of Illinois became the Democratic choice.

Change was everywhere.

In 1957, President Dwight Eisenhower set a milestone of sorts when he traveled to Camp David by helicopter, the first president to do so. The White House chose a Bell 2-seat H-13J helicopter to use for the flights. The first trips were piloted by Maj. Joseph E Barrett. The president arrived at 3:01 p.m. and motored to the main lodge where he practiced hitting golf balls until later in the day when the Eisenhowers and guests watched the movie "Big Land."

While the camp wasn't always so advanced in technology ---it took years to get a communications system to work to everyone's

satisfaction---the need to get from the camp to the White House in minutes instead of hours became urgent during the Cold War and, while it had been anticipated, there was concern over such details as to which helicopter to use and which branch of service would handle the mission. Today it's taken for granted. In the mid-1960s, the safety of the president was of primary importance after the assassination of John F. Kennedy. But even with the precautions, the presidential plans were put on hold when Mother Nature interfered. Some helicopter landings were forced to abruptly put down in Thurmont because of low clouds and fog. The president and guests were then transported to Camp David in limos.

Four years earlier Ike, Mamie and his mother in law Mrs. John Dowd, officially visited the camp for the first time on the weekend of the Fourth of July, six months after he became president. He handled communications with the White House and Seoul, Korea, about the ongoing Korean Conflict and then to the surprise of his hosts he took time to go next door to visit the Crippled Children's camp at Green Top. Ike was one of the few presidents to take time to drop in on the children. After spending about a half an hour with the kids, before he departed, he offered money for their dessert. Later, he was embarrassed when the wire services offered news stories about the "dessert." He felt that it was a private matter but he seemed unaware that as president he no longer had the shield of being a private citizen.

Travel time from Camp David to the South Lawn of the White House was approximately two hours by car caravan as the security people tried finding the fastest and most secure route. Normally, the president would travel on Rt.77 from Washington to Frederick, MD and take a variety of state routes to ensure that no pattern could be established on the way to the camp.

The chopper trip is approximately 30 minutes between the two points and describes a second reason for the transportation issue. Evacuating the president in a national emergency was always a priority, especially considering mountain weather which could turn to sleet, rain and fog in minutes and ground the helicopters. Urgency, said Jim Rowley, Secret Service president at the time, was important to the mission. The first official guest to the Catoctin resort was Nikita Khrushchev, chairman of the Council of Ministers of the USSR. But instead of clearing the air with the meeting, it caused confusion when the Soviet premier inserted a thought President Eisenhower later said was not accurate. Khruschev talked about a "Spirit of Camp David" which the US president denied. "I must say I never used it" and "it must mean that it looks like we can talk together without being mutually abusive."

Before he visited Eisenhower at the American "dacha," he asked his embassy in Washington to tell him what it was. "I couldn't find out for the life of me what this Camp David was. Not even the embassy understood. We were finally informed that Camp David was what we called a 'dacha,' a cabin in the mountains."

Security was a constant concern, said visitors and camp personnel because the site was still under the government's secrecy cloak and would stay so long after the war.

Franklin Delano Roosevelt's sudden death April 12, 1945 at 63, as the war in Europe was ending and the Pacific war grew more intense was a shock to many because the American people really didn't know how sick their president was. He had been criticized for running in a fourth term because the custom since George Washington was no more than three terms. He served an unprecedented 13 years in office.

His death was a shock to the Roosevelt Administration for the obvious reasons; FDR was a micro-manager who made final decisions even as he grew weaker. The Catoctin hideaway, for example, was virtually his retreat; no one else had the keys and few others knew about it. Maryland state officials were concerned about how much land would be needed for the FDR retreat specially if it was to get bigger.

Over the next few months details were worked out between Maryland and the federal government concerning how the land would be re-distributed.

Days later, staff at the camp was reduced to a maintenance contingent of about 20 men. Meanwhile, congress speculated on the future of the remote area.

There was one theory that said the installation was to be readied for the new president with no delays. Others were interested in selling the retreat claiming the US government had no business offering the president, his family and friends a personal gift of property to use. What evolved was a difference of opinion among democrats.

Truman was unaware of the development of the atomic bomb and was also without knowledge of Shangri-La. He never visited the secret place although some Roosevelt staff members were there

President Truman was so concerned with austerity and budget problems he took the view that "if it ain't broke don't fix it. "But Mamie Eisenhower felt there had to be more than upkeep and in 1959 she set out to make the improvements.

frequently. He was supposedly never invited. At the same time, he made it clear when he discovered FDR's hideaway that such things didn't interest him. In deference to FDR who chose him vice president, Truman proposed the retreat become a shrine to give recognition to those who fought in the war. He wrote to Maryland Gov. Hubert R. O'Connor: "I have decided because of the historical events of national and international interest now associated with the Catoctin Recreational Area that this should  be retained by the Federal Government and made a part of the National Park Service of the Department of the Interior. This action is in accord with the position expressed by the late President Roosevelt before his death."

During the war, a 130 man Marine detachment handled security 24 hours a day. "At the close of WWII the Marine unit departed the area and it was replaced by two sailors, one at the gate and one duty petty officer inside the camp. The gate sentry

The Trumans had shown movies but nothing like the Eisenhowers who were first generation picture buffs. The Eisenhowers brought a movie projector and within months Camp David had a Hollywood screening theater with privacy for guest and family.

was armed with a .45 pistol. After a couple of mishaps in 1956 the bullets were taken away. You can bet that the Marine sentries that patrol the area now carry live ammunition!" But there was another reason for a weapon in those early days; poisonous snakes such as copperheads and timber rattlers also inhabited the mountains, too.

The Eisenhowers were the more energetic of the first presidents in upgrading the camp. President Truman was so concerned with austerity and budget problems he took the view that "if it ain't broke don't fix it." But Mamie Eisenhower felt there had to be more than upkeep and in 1959 she set out to make the improvements.

The couple must have had interesting discussions about the work because the general took over an administration short on cash. Two baths and a partial bath were built just off the living area of the main lodge. A hallway was also added and the lower terrace was added. A central air conditioning system was installed in the main lodge which was thought to be a luxury by military people who weren't used to such luxuries.

The Trumans had shown movies but nothing like the Eisenhowers who were first generation picture buffs. The Eisenhowers brought a movie projector and within months Camp David had a Hollywood screening theater with privacy for guest and family. The screen operates electronically and to save space, drops from the ceiling.

Just around the corner was the screened in sun porch which was enlarged. It provided a spectacular panoramic view of the Monocacy Valley. The porch was screened until the Truman Administration and then it was updated for year-round use.

In making changes some items were lost. . . for good. There had been pen and ink drawings of sailing ships celebrating British defeats at sea during the Revolution and the War of 1812. They were thought to have been memories of the president's years as assistant secretary of the Navy. The drawings were discovered missing and probably lost during the Eisenhower years.

It's generally known that Ike, like a number of presidents, was an avid golfer. One staffer I talked to suggested that had Ike arrived at Camp David earlier there might have been an 18-hole course surrounding the mountain retreat not a 4 pitch and putt inside. Yet one man's joy in playing the game was another's indifference. On the Chris Matthews TV show in early 2013, President Barack Obama told a national audience he didn't like going to Camp David because it doesn't have a course. . .it has only a putting green!

According to reporters who cover the president, the evidence is in his visits to the camp. Mark Knoller, a CBS White House reporter who has tracked the president's vacation days, notes that Obama journeyed to the camp 29 times, accounting for 72 days or about 5 percent of his term. By contrast, President George W Bush went to Camp David 149 times over 487 days.

President Eisenhower's passion for golf created the first miniature course on federal land in 1955 when the media displayed a four-hole one green design by golfing legend Bobby Jones and funded by Ike's friends. The caveat in the four hole cluster was that each of the holes was replica of favorite greens at the Augusta National and Burning Tree golf courses. In a story prepared by Herbert Warren Wind in Sports Illustrated magazine, the noted writer creates a colorful word picture of the pitch and putt course: "There is a terrace in front, and then the land slopes quickly down to a small clearing that was devised by President Roosevelt so that a person lolling on the terrace could command a super view of the countryside on a clear day, a 30 to 40 mile vista. From the terrace to the edge of the wood line, measures about 140 yards and runs to about the same yardage in width." It was hardly enough room for one good golf hole. It was a challenge that Jones couldn't pass up. He enjoyed the puzzle of spatial problems in golf. His answer? He created four tees by the right hand edge of the green. The first 100 yards from the hole and 15 feet above the level of the green. The second was 140 yards away and 20 feet above. The third was 120 yards and 20 feet below and the fourth was 80 yards away from the hole and 15 feet below the tee. Said Wind in his evaluation of the pitch and putt at Camp David "It offers a splendid variety of shots and no confusion in a foursome as long as each player uses clearly distinguishable set of balls like the ones imprinted with MR. PRESIDENT." The par for each hole is 3.

No question the Eisenhowers brought with them the dawn of a new era to the Catoctin Mountains. The credit, a number of friends and observers said, should go to Mamie. Days after Attorney General Herbert Brownell and his assistant Warren Burger visited Camp David to assess whether the new president should dispose of the property or not, they sent a mock petition for clemency for the site inferring that the general feeling was that some wondered why the government would keep such a property with no redeeming value.

Ike, said several observers, approached the presidency as he did a military campaign. He quickly noted the need for a budget curb and the staggering cost of wartime government he inherited. Dwight' s grandson David told author Dale Nelson the president thought the camp was becoming "too lavish." But good friend George Allen of the Washington football dynasty advised the president to take his family and visit the Catoctin site before making a decision.

Mamie persisted. The camp was an ideal place for fishing, boating and a variety of other sports but it desperately needed refurbishing and remodeling. Where would the money come from given the government's financial predicament? It was the Navy Department that responded. The problem said a member of the president's staff was that there was no line item for improvements especially at a time when the president was calling for cuts elsewhere. David said he thought his grandfather would close it. But Mamie argued that the camp was important historically and an ideal place to welcome the golfing world.

She was told informally that getting the general's support was imperative. She used the "hint" persistently and, in time, renovations were made. She didn't limit her requests to furniture and kitchen utensils either. She made pleas for shrubbery, general upkeep and reconstruction. Her "hints" led to more changes at the retreat than previous administrations had made.

The Eisenhowers loved to be outdoors as often as possible in good weather so to improve the opportunity to eat outside they added a flagstone terrace and a cooking pavilion beside the Main Lodge. Ike enjoyed cooking too, so having a hamburger prepared by the commander in chief was a special treat.

When it came to exclusive golf courses few topped the four hole Camp David course. According to a Sports Illustrated article, the developers of the short game, the McDonald Design Group of Jessup, had exactly 140 yards to use to construct holes beside the lodge. When you have the possibility of new owners or tenants every four years you have to think out of the box to make it work. For example, President Bill Clinton kept hitting the above ground fueling system with his drive near the helicopter landing zone during his tenure. After striking it twice on one hole he complained that the fueling system should have been put underground. Later, the apparatus was put in the ground. But no one has mentioned if it aided his game.

Times were changing on the mountaintop and in the nation. In the final year of Truman's presidency for example, the Congress and state governments passed the 22nd Amendment which limited the president to only two terms. Roosevelt's unprecedented four terms and death in office caused concern as the public became aware of how precarious it was with an incapacitated leader. Change was everywhere. The first commercial color television broadcast was made by Columbia Broadcasting which spent $15 million over 11 years to perfect the technology on June 25, 1951. The first digital computer built for commercial purposes by UNIVAC came just several weeks earlier.

While neither had immediate impact, their existence and growth fueled the American economy and the American way of life.

Ike didn't appreciate those who didn't follow the rules. The USBC Combat Helicopter Association tells the story of a veteran Korean War FAU pilot who landed on top of Ike's putting green. The Association said "the pilot was called in immediately when he returned to Quantico. The president didn't take kindly to people disrupting his tranquility or damaging his golf course. No additional information was released about the pilot.

One of the most valued perks of the presidency, according to George Bush Jr., was having Camp David for rest and relaxation. Thanks to the Eisenhowers it has retained its values and traditions. There never was a set of instructions that went with the place. But Mamie and Ike decided to make it a livable residence and a respected place for world leaders to meet, to mingle and talk.

The Catoctin Mountain chalet was seen more as a fixture in their household when Ike suffered a heart attack and was confined to bed rest. He spent most of his recovery time at Aspen Lodge.

His first cabinet meeting was held August 13, 1954, and he invited the entire staff to Camp David and virtually turned the secret hideaway over to them to use. It was a step neither Roosevelt nor Truman had taken and it was well received. Imagine a group of camp aides and their families fishing for trout, shooting skeet or engaging in a modified golf match on Ike' s four hole course. Former camp administrator Bill King remembers how affable Ike

Thanks to the Eisenhowers it has retained its values and traditions. There never was a set of instructions that went with the place. But Mamie and Ike decided to make it a livable residence and a respected place for world leaders to meet, with dignity yet casualness, to discuss world affairs.

was when he saw how staff members enjoyed relaxing and playing at the retreat. He also remembered an incident that occurred to him while working with the president. He had been sent to the Eisenhower farm on an errand "Ike came out to greet us and ask us to get our shotguns and join him in pheasant hunting. We were walking down the corn field rows with Ike in the middle and we were separated by 20 yards each. A pheasant got up in front of me and flew off. Ike called over and asked me why I didn't shoot. I told him the pheasant had scared the hell out of me! The truth was my shotgun wasn't loaded! Somewhere in my mind when I started to load the gun I could see the headlines in the next day's paper saying: 'Dumb Sailor Shoots President: Insists It was an Accident!' I quickly put the shells in my pocket."

In the days before the non-denominational Evergreen Chapel was built, the Eisenhowers were reluc-

tant to provide advance information to media about
the church services they
planned to attend. No
reason was given although
it was assumed that they
felt it was a private matter. While at Camp David,
they attended the Trinity
United Church of Christ in

Thurmont. No special attention was given to them when they attended and that pleased the president. They entertained on the
Camp David patio playing Scrabble or mind games. On other
occasions they read. And then there were times when they simply
did nothing. The late historian Stephen Ambrose in his 1964 book
Eisenhower: The President said that Ike and Mamie could sit for
an hour or two without conversation.

Meanwhile, camp communication personnel increased from
several persons to 20 and two additional rooms were added to
Hickory Lodge to house the new people. King remembered that
when he was on the mountaintop the staff "was selected on the
basis of service records." The military personnel were all carefully
selected from US bases around the globe.

The Cold War continued unabated with both sides sparring
for ways to glean information from the other. In early April, 1954,
Eisenhower following advice from the state department regarding Russian belligerence gave America its first nuclear defense, a
3,000 mile early warning radar net across Canada's north to protect both countries. Several years earlier, a lone military operator
handled the growing amount of traffic but by the mid-1950s the
volume of telegrams had significantly increased demanding improvement. At the same time, 4,400 acres of land was transferred
to the State of Maryland where it expanded Cunningham Falls

State Park. The same year, the National Park Service approved the renaming of Catoctin Recreational Demonstration Area to Catoctin Mountain Park and Congress approved authority to exchange lands to consolidate holdings in the park.

The renaming was important to clear up the misunderstandings and misperceptions that confused mountain residents, government officials and visitors. Said de Teel Patterson, acting associate director of cultural resources for the National Park Service at the time, "The proximity of Catoctin Mountain Park, Camp

> *Catoctin Mountain Park is continually misunderstood as being closed to the public because of the presence of Camp David. Renaming the park as a 'national recreation area' would offer an opportunity to reintroduce the park as an area that is open to public recreation."*

David and Cunningham Falls State Park has caused longstanding confusion for visitors to the area. Catoctin Mountain Park is continually misunderstood as being closed to the public because of the presence of Camp David. Renaming the park as a 'national recreation area' would offer an opportunity to reintroduce the park as an area that is open to public recreation."

Spring, 1955, brought more technology to the camp to ease and speed visitors back and forth. A heliport, built outside the camp fence during the last year or two of the Roosevelt years, was merely a clearing that the crew made into a baseball diamond. By the end of 1955, the clearing had been enlarged, a hangar built and a skeet range constructed.

While the Eisenhower farm was called the "temporary White House" during his two terms, helicopters played a significant role in transporting people to and from the camp, farm and the White House. Bill King recalls the friendly competition between the Marines and the Army over which branch of the service would provide transport at Camp David. "The Marines won and Executive Flight Detachment at Bowling Green, went out. But I don't

recall any traffic jams in the mountain after that. From the amount of traffic around camp in those days, it would be hard to create a traffic jam, really," King said with a broad smile.

Helicopters were considered strictly for transportation but some groundskeepers thought the blades could be used to blow away the canopy of leaves as summer turned to fall in the Adirondacks and the Catoctin Mountains. That brought a reaction, too, he said. "The National Park Service raised hell about them. But that wasn't my way of solving the problem. They wouldn't let me cut down any live trees but to me they all looked dead. That was the way I thought I could control the leaf problem. Each year, however, we cut down a few dead trees. The leaves though were a real problem. For example, at the swimming pools you could throw a handful of leaves in the pool and they would use up all of the chlorine," the camp administrator said.

Groundskeepers were constantly dealing with the problem of trying to live and work in a remote and rustic region without much backup. Getting city people to understand that the camp uses septic systems and wells and did not have a public utility has always been difficult.

Even acts of appreciation could bring headaches, King discovered. "A contractor wanted to give something to his crew for their effort. We came up with two half kegs of beer. The base commander and I talked it over and decided to sell the beer on two afternoons. When we had gotten the 2nd keg we had enough to buy three more kegs! So much for trying to do a good deed!" Bill said with a smile. "We were going to sell beer to the crew once a week. We were able to pay the bartender but I took no money. Someone in the State Department told me not to charge for the beer or other items. I was going to get things on credit but they were all in my name. By the time Khrushchev left for Russia, I was about two months pay in debt! It took me over two months to get the State Department to send me a check for the balance!" he said.

In the spring, 1957, newly appointed British Prime Minister Harold MacMillan became the first head of state to journey to Camp David for a visit and a talk with Eisenhower. The president and the prime minister met at the White House and spent the weekend in the Catoctin Mountains. They discussed the extension of the Truman Plan and the formation of the Eisenhower Doctrine as well as Anglo-American friendship. Unlike earlier days church attendance at the Trinity United Church in Thurmont brought together representatives of the US Secret Service and Scotland Yard. At the time, Thurmont had no police chief so the group had to meet with the village mayor to organize the motorcade that was planned. It went well and both MacMillan and Eisenhower returned to camp after church and finished the details. The MacMillan-Eisenhower sessions were considered the longest conference held during the president's tenure.

The Army and Marine helicopter detachments assigned to the Catoctin Mountain helicopter pad were now considered safe by the Secret Service (such aircraft was still in its infancy in the 1950s) after both Scotland Yard and the US Service had conducted their own exams. Camp David veterans remember that the helicopter crews that flew into the camp wanted their beer cool on hot summer nights. "Things were still quite casual and trial and error. Anyway, cooling the beer quickly became a problem until

we came up with the idea of using the large CO2 fire extinguishers," said one of the participants. Of course, the CO2 flat 'killed' grass on the lawn! Picture a green lawn with a brown oval in it with a green rectangle the approximate size of a beer case in the middle of the oval. It was impossible to explain the next day when questions were raised!" King said.

Renovations at Camp David began in 1958 when a detachment of Seabees showed up to assist camp regulars. "One of the first projects was to drain the septic tank in front of the camp commander's lodge. It had been a problem spot for years. The young ensign asked what should be done about it. I gave him two answers: 1. Redo the drain field or 2. Run the line down the hill to the system that served Aspen (main lodge). I told him that he would have to dig the trench by hand because a back hoe would tear up too much and kill a lot of trees. The ensign decided on the back hoe and he suffered the consequences. When the commander saw the trench he went nuts! King said he was so angry he confined the ensign to quarters."

Former Camp David administrator King said the Khruschev visit in September, 1959, was the most important event in his tenure on the mountain. It was a most hectic weekend. "We had more people aboard than one could find a bunk for. We rented rooms in the Cozy Inn Thurmont. The problem though was transportation to and from the town. It was eight miles away. Everybody pitched in and we made it work."

You had to be flexible to handle a Camp David assignment, King added. "We did things and we worked together as a team. I remember we had a German delegation here twice and a Russian group too. It was an exciting time to be on the mountain and in world affairs."

At the same time Camp David was where Murphy's Law was written, said a number of sailors. For example, when there were guests visiting Laurel Cabin, the chief would call and tell the steward to mix a batch of drinks in case some of the guests wanted one for the road. No one questioned the order. As all the guests left, it was made sure that the mixed drinks were disposed of, too. No one wanted to see good wine liquor go to waste! Little government booze ever went down the drain!

Ike added to the excitement and demonstrated his own creativity. A painter, he found pastoral scenes at the camp and his farm which satisfied his creativity needs. He continued working to let others see the beauty he saw in the American countryside.

By the time Ike left office there were 64 members of his crew on board with one Marine security office. There had been a growth of 14 during his eight years of extended service.

Bibliography
Interview with Jerry Freeze, owner of The Cozy Inn; Bill King, Camp David administrator;
Web: A guided Tour of Camp David(no longer available)
The President Is At Camp David by Dale Nelson
Commander's Notes, circa 1950s
by the WPA in 1935. It opened in 1938 originally to be used by federal government agents and their families under the guidance of the WPA. In 1942 President Roosevelt converted it to a retreat.

by John "Jack" Behrens

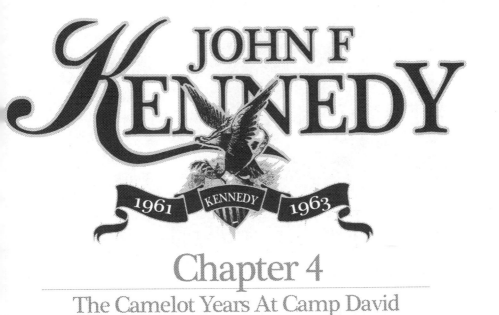

JOHN F KENNEDY

1961 · KENNEDY · 1963

Chapter 4

The Camelot Years At Camp David

John F. "Jack" Kennedy was one of those persons who could bring excitement to a room, a floor or a convention hall by entering it. He did that at the Democratic Convention in Los Angeles when he swept the nomination from Lyndon Johnson and Adlai Stevenson on the first ballot in 1960.

His style was smooth and talented and his youth and his credentials overshadowed any negatives. Not many young men had written books about courage and excited the political elite of the nation as he had. Recognizing his interest in history, Rep. Charles McC. Mathias, whose congressional district included the Catoctin Mountain area, spent an afternoon with the Kennedys examining some of the historical sites. Later in his term, he visited the battlefields at Gettysburg and Antietam.

The country was beginning the Camelot Years, a time for fresh thoughts, a cleansing of old politics and the re-birth of sophistication. The campaign that year was highlighted by four television debates be-tween Kennedy and Vice President Richard Nixon, the Republi-can nominee. It was the first time the public could see and hear candidates exchange views in their homes across the country. It was the year of the television debate.

The public didn't really understand the severity of the back pain that cause Jack Kennedy to grimace when sitting in any chair because it wasn't always mentioned. The pain was so severe at times that Kennedy's favorite rocker was put in the middle of the front row of the White House's Family Theater so he could see films. He also had an orthopedic bed set up in the theater room

so he could watch propped up on the bed, if he chose. What caused his pain? Typically, there were differ-ent theories. It was known that he suffered from coli-tis, prostatitis and Addi-son's disease among the more prominent illnesses. The most logical was pain caused by the difference in the length of his legs. His afflictions caused him to be unable to perform simple tasks like pulling his shoe and sock on his left foot. He took as many as 12 medications at once and he took more when stressed.

The Kennedys were certain that they wouldn't have to use Camp David if elected because they had Hyannis on the Cape, among other vacation locations to go to as a family, and they enjoyed their outings and competition among themselves. The family would go to Palm Beach in the winter and Hyannis and Newport on special holidays, said Kennedy friend Arthur Schlesinger Jr., in his book, One Thousand Days. "The Kennedys liked to preserve

The constant concern was for the president and his family's safety. "About the only place the president and his family were totally safe was at the mountain retreat." Because it is a military reservation the press was permitted on the grounds only when invited.

weekends as much as possible for themselves and their children. In 1961, they took a house at Glen Orr, VA but the president felt he was confined." The constant concern was for the president and his family's safety. "About the only place the president and his family were totally safe was at the mountain retreat." Because it is a military reservation the press was permitted on the grounds only when invited. The policy hasn't changed although the government has given more liberty in arranging special interviews with media and celebrated media people.

It didn't take Mrs. Kennedy long to fall in love with Camp David. The freedom and privacy she and her children had was priceless, she told friends. While at the camp she could move around without drawing a crowd. Even Secret Service agents stayed out of sight. As important to her was the stable that had been added to ensure that she and her daughter could ride their horses, Tartar and Macaroni. She also discovered how close she

was to many of the stores she enjoyed. Camp staff reported that she occasionally drove herself to Thurmont and shopped. Caroline and John enjoyed Fantasyland in nearby Gettysburg and she took them a number of times.

Those who visited the mountain hideaway were impressed with the security measures to protect the president and his family. Here's how Woody Ryder IV described wrong turns that put him right at the camp front door: "When I was a student at Gettysburg College my roommate and I used to drive from Gettysburg south on US 15 to Emmetsburg, MD. You could get beer and wine in MD but PA held the line at 21. We'd often get lost around Thurmont. On a few occasions, we'd make a wrong turn. All of a sudden on the right we'd see multiple-tiers of chainlink fence and some ominous US government signs 'Absolutely No Parking' or

'No Standing at Any Time'." We'd continue up further only to see on the right what could have passed for a wooden entry sign at some Pocono or Adirondack resort, but all it said was 'Camp David.' The checkpoint Charlie type of booth that told you unless you had the right kind of ID or you were a reincarnation of Fala you'd better not try to scamper. If there was a car behind you... you were already too late to escape!"

The Obama Administration worked with world media to cover the largest event in Camp history when it welcomed heads of state of the Big Eight for the Big Eight Summit in May, 2012. It's more the reason all presidents sought the shelter of the Catoctin Mountain retreat at some point during their tenure in the White House. From Richard Nixon to George W. Bush, some presidents think they can control events because of their power. Others have tried and failed. But, you can control location and ambiance with a powerful tool like Camp David.

> *And what about Camp David, a reporter asked? "I don't plan to use Camp David very often. I will keep Camp David ... but, I doubt if I will go there very often," JF K replied. He should have checked with Jackie. Just a few months later her horse and Carolyn's pony made their way to the Catoctin Mountains and weekends were busier at Camp David.*

When you enter the gates at the camp, your world has changed. Just look around and you know why. You are protected by the best security systems the US government can buy. No one has penetrated the network, although there have been numerous accidental intrusions because of the heightened security overhead as well as on the ground. Following the assassination of JFK, security on the 125 acre retreat was increased and kept on high alert for a period of time. The Secret Service reported that at "least a couple of dozen incidents have occurred around Camp David and Washington since 9-11" although most of them have gone unreported and not resulted in the scrambling of fighter jets. Observers say the Secret Service will detain those without a credible explanation or answer for their actions. Several months after he was chosen as the 35th president of the United States, John F. Kennedy told reporters at his first major press conference that he "had no plans to use the two government owned yachts then in service." And what about Camp David, a reporter asked? "I don't

plan to use Camp David very often. I will keep Camp David...but, I doubt if I will go there very often," JFK replied. He should have checked with Jackie. Just a few months later her horse and Caroline's pony made their way to the Catoctin Mountains and weekends were busier at Camp David.

There's a proud tradition that the Secret Service always observes. The Secret Service will always have the president's "back." Secret Service spokesman Jim Macklin said the service takes every incursion as a serious matter.

Mrs. Kennedy was unlike Mamie and Bess Truman in many ways. All had their strengths but Jackie was more cultured. Her background was upper class. She was used to asking for staff help whether it be to get a gown from the closet or rearranging the room. But while the president was attempting to talk about frugality publicly she was sending a driver to Washington each afternoon to pick up the late Washington paper. The driver for the White House figured a way to drive to Hagerstown to get the paper from a commuter flight pilot instead of driving to Washington. All he had to pay was the price of the paper.

It was going well until an article appeared in the Washington Post and it mentioned that a rival paper was being picked up for Mrs. Kennedy. A district congressman called to raise hell about

the cost and unfairness of "chartering" a plane (which didn't oc-
cur) for the Kennedys. The deliveries stopped the same day.

Shortly after the Kennedys
traveled to the camp, someone
threw a rock in the pond in front
of Aspen Lodge and staff members
became fearful that the young Kennedy children might get hurt. So,
to be cautious and safe, the staff
drained the pond! The reason,
of course, was that there was no
lifeguard on duty and worse, the
banks of the pond could be treacherous. Thus began the odyssey
of Camelot 1963.

Kennedy and his family enjoyed the recreation sites at Camp
David although Jack said it wouldn't be used. They loved football
in the front lawn with most of the family participating. News
cameras would frequently catch a pickup game with a number
of the family involved. The president and his wife began to use
the camp in the spring of 1963 when he had a bridle path cleared

> *Shortly after the Kennedys traveled to the camp, some-*
> *one threw a rock in the pond in front of Aspen Lodge and*
> *staff members became fearful that the young Kennedy*
> *children might get hurt. So, to be cautious and safe, the*
> *staff drained the pond!*

along the outer perimeter of the camp. A stable was also built and
a pony ring for Caroline's pony, Macaroni. The family enjoyed
riding on weekends after that. Crew members remember the gift
presented to her by the king of Morocco; an ornamental saddle.
The king was most impressed by the US president. To make life
more comfortable for the president who suffered from a chronic

back, a rocking chair was added to the sun porch as a gift from the king. The monarch had called Camp David to inquire about Kennedy. The president's bad back caused the staff concern. He wanted the swimming pool heated above 100F degrees daily.

Bill King and other staff members fully cooperated with the president. King walked the camp early every morning to make sure nothing was out of place. One morning, the camp administrator said, "as I approached the pool I could see that something was clearly wrong. The tar that was in pool joints was melting and floating to the surface. The thermostat had quit, we discovered, and failed to close the steam valve. Heat was boiling the joints. We tried to add fresh water to float off the tar and cool the pool, but it didn't work."

The steam line to the pool and the heating system were oversized because camp officials wanted to have the option of raising the temperature of the pool within four hours, King explained.

Camp personnel still talk about good intentions that turn sour during those years. For example, the time Robert Kennedy called saying he wanted to go swimming. "I told him our pool was full of leaves and ice but I would see if there was an indoor pool nearby. He said he didn't want an indoor pool. The only thing I could think of was the hole at the Crows Nest. I called the Crows

Nest and told them that we had a party of people that would like to come to swim and that he should have some cookies and something to drink at the lodge. We agreed on a price of $25."

A guide took Robert to the Nest. As the group left singing rag top with the top down, the feeling was that they would hit the pond full of freshly melted snow which should wake them quickly.

"I didn't hear more about it until the Crows Nest sent me a bill for $50. I called and discovered that the group was there…twice! When Robert left camp to return to Washington, they stopped at the Crows Nest and went swimming again!"

At about that time the Camp was given horses from the Marines. They were named after the WWII battles of Tarawa and Guadalcanal. "We built a stable for them and cleared a path through the woods for them," King continued. "That's how we got Tartar and Macaroni", he said. JFK was building a house on Rattlesnake Mountain or someplace and had let the lease on Glen Oar expire. To the Kennedys' credit, they paid for their horse feed bills. On the other hand, the Camp didn't know who was going to pay and didn't want to send the president a bill!"

It was a different matter with Caroline's room. A female interior decorator finished the room. But Jackie called and wanted to add another chair for the bedroom suite. Said Bill King, "We got a hold of the decorator and she said she had dealt with the factory. We didn't know if we'd match the chair and the decorator arranged for it to be sent to Camp David. As it turned out, two drivers left the Camp for North Carolina to get the chair for Mrs. Kennedy but, unfortunately, she had already decided against the Camp David chair. It was important, though, to let donors know your plans."

The camp had its own volunteer fire brigade. Every camp in Catoctin Mountains was self-contained with wells or ponds to supply drinking water and potable water for sanitation. At Camp David, a water system was designed so that, if a hydrant was opened, pumps came on to build the pressure to above 100 pounds per inch. "Our system wasn't working because unless you had a fire hose open to keep the pressure down, the pumps built up pressure and cut off. Pumps would just keep cutting on and off," said camp administrator, Bill King.

"One night, the store room, which included the carpenter shop, the plumbing shop and the electrical shop, caught fire. I think the first thing that happened was the fire fighters opened the

hydrant, the pumps came on and busted the fire main. When the spot where the main ruptured was dug out, it was found the pipe was in contact with the rock. That's where I got gray hairs working at Camp David," he added. My relief was at the Camp which gave me confidence as he was learning the ropes. I sat down with him and marveled at how far we had come in a short while.

They were to have no visitors and a peaceful time in the final weeks. It didn't turn out that the way but, then, that's the truth wherever you are. All was fine. Young people who marry and leave home know the harshness of finding a place to live. The young Kennedys endured something similar. According to Pierre Salinger in his book, With Kennedy, the president and his new wife had no place outside the capital to stay but Camp David. While he had ruled out the Catoctin Mountains in the beginning, they started visiting the retreat and liked it more and more. Salinger wrote: "it was actually the perfect place for the president. You had a beautiful house, with all the necessary communication equipment built in. Next door to the house was a (modified) golf course, a swimming pool, a bowling alley, a basketball court, a skeet range and ample grounds for horses to romp. The view from the house of the surrounding Catoctin Mountains was breath-taking, particularly in the spring and fall. And, of course, you could be sure that no photographers were hiding in the trees."

The crew at the mountain anticipated the arrival of a more athletic family than the previous occupants when, in the early 1960s, two tennis courts were rebuilt at Camp David, Bill King remembers. The original courts were constructed of a substance like a green floor sweeping compound. "It was a pain in the butt and it scarred easily. The crew had to keep it damp or it would turn into fine green dust. The courts were completely rebuilt with donated funds. There are two regulation clay courts now." King, who left

The crew at the mountain anticipated the arrival of a more athletic family than the previous occupants when, in the early 1960s, two tennis courts were rebuilt at Camp David.

with a 13 year tenure at the mountain retreat in June 1963, remembered that Kennedy had a short visit with his successor about the secret Bay of Pigs matter, but we didn't see him for a while after that. However, after the stable lease ran out for Mrs. Kennedy's horse Tartar and Caroline's pony, the Kennedys made several visits. The former camp administrator believes the whole Kennedy family got together once at the mountaintop before Jack's death.

Among the visitors to Camp David in the summer of '63 was the John Glenn family.

"I remember that someone had given John 22 rifles and the group went to the town dump to shoot some targets. It was the first time I saw a plastic stock used," stated King. They had varying opinions about the stock but they enjoyed the practice rounds. The shooters were on target and the scores said that it was a good afternoon on the range.

While security remained tight while the president was at the camp, Salinger made one change in the coverage. "I allowed  the photographers when the president was at Camp David into the preserve as far as the helicopter landing pad so they could personally observe that the president and his family had arrived. They were then ushered off the premises." The Kennedys, unlike their elder presidential predecessors, needed a sanctuary from the public. While at the camp, Mrs. Kennedy was able to move around more without drawing a crowd. Even the Secret Service would stay out of sight," said King.

"I recall that may have been the only time that Ted Kennedy was there, but Robert and his clan were there several times. There were several meetings by different groups and several of the cabinet," said King.

During the Kennedys tenure at Camp David, the recreational facilities were heavily used. And the Kennedys discovered they were close to many sights and nearby communities as well as a

number of stores. "It was not unusual for Mrs. Kennedy to drive to Thurmont and do her shopping. Fantasyland Park in Gettysburg was a favorite spot for John Jr. and Caroline. Mrs. Kennedy took them to that children's park on a number of occasions, King continued. "But, there was always the threat that the media would soon arrive and cause chaos." said Bill King. The bigger threat was a member of the media being invited along and writing about what they saw. It happened. "She took the threat seriously. You had such a short time span to make such decisions. I can remember when Walter Winchell would come to camp and we would hide all the new things and put the junk on display. He used to spend his time looking around the area. He was allowed to visit and take a few notes and you knew he was looking for the things that could raise eyebrows and blood pressure."

Winchell was well known as a columnist with 2,000 newspapers and more than 50 million readers. His Sunday night radio broadcast was listened to by 20 million and powered his strength in media. He attacked personalities as well as organizations, but in his early days, he was an intimate friend of known gangsters.

Even in the murky field of journalism of the day, his methods of gathering information weren't ethical. He was, however, one of the first media personalities to openly attack Nazi leader Adolph Hitler.

Ask any camp regular about the Detex Watch Clock but stand a few feet back in case his temper mounts! There are probably more stories about how young seamen remember the infernal security alarm. Its purpose, since it came out 90 years ago, has been to make sure guards do their jobs and perimeters are secure. Today, they are shoulder mounted, hand held and completely moveable. The watch can be the independent alert to protect the guard

and the property. One thing for sure, you could toss that thing 200 or more feet in the air or bounce it off the ground and it would still keep working!

If the Kennedys were at the camp on a Sunday, you would find them at the Recreation Hall, in Hickory Hall, which had been converted into a chapel and Mass was celebrated for Catholic worshippers with Rev John J. MacNulty from nearby Fort Richie, MD. Servicemen from the Navy and Marine Corps and their families were invited along with others from the area. It was thought the house in the Rattlesnake region that the family was building in West Virginia attracted new parishioners.

Leaves were a continuing problem with the brass at Camp David. They probably are to every homeowner, too. But when

...they went about the drudgery of reducing mountains of leaves weekly in the fall. The staff even talked to chopper pilots about flying lower over the camp to blow the leaves in one direction and make it easier for removing them.

you're in charge of 125 acres of land covered by trees and you have bosses determined to keep things neat, clean and orderly the battle can become insane! That's what the enlisted personnel felt as they went about the drudgery of reducing mountains of leaves weekly in the fall. The staff even talked to chopper pilots about flying lower over the camp to blow the leaves in one direction and make it easier for removing them. There were actually several times when groups of the enlisted ran around with baskets trying to catch the leaves. It actually happened! One staffer said if he had his way, more trees would be cut down. Less leaves! The leaves were a real problem for nearly everyone. The doctor was always getting water samples to determine the chlorine levels because it only took a few to contaminate a pool.

by John "Jack" Behrens

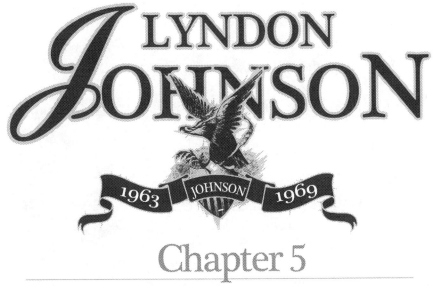

LYNDON JOHNSON

1963 · JOHNSON · 1969

Chapter 5

Lyndon Johnson's Confidence Sometimes Surpassed Reality, Common Sense

I met him on the campaign trail in 1974 shortly after I had joined an Ohio Democratic candidate for the House as legislative aide. Lyndon Johnson was exuberant and coarse at the same time in that slurpy southern twang that identified his heritage. "You could do so much better joining my crowd, son. You don't have anything in common with those country boys," he smiled. I spent the next four years getting to see the good, bad and sometimes ugly side of the man they call LBJ. Cutting through the black as tar exterior to find the real Lyndon Johnson wasn't easy, though.

Like his predecessor Johnson was skeptical of how he would use Camp David once it became his to visit. But unlike the former White House occupants, he had been to the Camp David several times before. He still liked his ranch. He saw the camp as a

He saw the camp as a place for he and Ladybird to meet foreign dignitaries when they came to town. "Why else would I want to go there?" he asked me expecting no answer.

place for he and Lady Bird to meet foreign dignitaries when they came to town. "Why else would I want to go there?" he asked me expecting no answer.

In his book With Kennedy, Pierre Salinger told of how the family made changes at the camp while they were there. They got rid of a large amount of the original camp furniture. "It was uncomfortable," he said years later at a press conference. "I wish we would have known... we would have liked to have had it," said Jerry Freeze owner of nearby Cozy Country Inn, Thurmont. Actually, it went back in the federal attic where much of it came from.

...the family made changes at the camp while they were there. They got rid of a large amount of the original camp furniture. "It was uncomfortable," he said years later at a press conference.

Johnson had been to the camp as Vice President several times visiting in an official capacity but one of his memorable trips to the area came a few months after he became President. He didn't come to visit

Camp David; however, he came to visit the first Job Corps Center in the country just down the road. He spent a few hours with the young men participating in one of his Great Society programs. Later, he went to Camp David for dinner with his military and foreign affairs advisers who had made the trip from Washington.

Many historians and even Johnson claimed he wasn't really interested in the camp at the mountaintop, but camp crew saw a different side. People close to him got the feeling he found it awkward wandering around in a rustic lodge that was more a resort than a meeting place. Johnson even took a sampling of his staff as to whether the camp should be kept a federal retreat or not, said William White in his book. Lyndon B. Johnson, the President, put everyone on notice his first trip to the camp that he required a vast amount of energy from those around him. His energy level was surprising. The first time he bowled at the camp he knocked down seven pins, not the ten required for a strike. Unhappy with his attempt at playing the game he carefully sighted down his arm, readjusted his stance and pointed the ball like a weapon. His second throw was a winner. "A strike Mr. President," said the attendant. But no record remains to tell us how the game ended. In A Guided Tour of Camp David he told staff he enjoyed the place. He visited Camp David 29 times in his five years and 6 months in the White House.

His energy level was surprising. The first time he bowled at the camp he knocked down seven pins not the ten required for a strike. Unhappy with his attempt at playing the game he carefully sighted down his arm, readjusted his stance and pointed the ball like a weapon. His second throw was a winner. "A strike Mr. President," said the attendant. But no record remains to tell us how the game ended.

While Johnson wanted everybody to believe that his way was the best for the country and friends, the intimacy of Camp David didn't always work.

When political demonstrations at the White House became loud and disturbing to the thin-skinned LBJ, he would climb into his Marine One helicopter and fly off to the camp for "a clear view of national horizons."

Mrs. Johnson, meanwhile, wanted to take the cold, damp mountain air out of any cabin she visited when in the Catoctins. "I recall several visits by Vice President Johnson but only one when Lady Bird came along. There are several large fireplaces in camp and they put smoke out until the fireplace got hot. I used to lay logs on the fireplace until it got hot. Lady Bird had the dining room table moved near the fireplace and during the meal she would invariably ask that the fire be lit. Mistake!" laughed Bill King. "It would warm up considerably!"

> *I recall several visits by Vice President Johnson but only one when Lady Bird came along.*

Then there was the time the president checked into the camp and brought along his private secretary. We suggested his secretary could be housed in Witch Hazel Lodge which was unoccupied at the time. The president said no he thought it best to put her in Aspen Lodge (the president's private lodge) because he had a few personal letters to be written early in the day. Next morning, the president asked that the secretary handle the task. Later in the day, Johnson became alarmed when he couldn't find her and shouted for security to 'close the gate.' Don't let anyone out! Get a search party...my secretary is missing!"

Someone suggested searching all the cabins but wiser heads prevailed. What if a young sailor was found somewhere he shouldn't be, doing something he knew he shouldn't be doing. You get the picture. The Marines, at the

same time, were sent into the woods to search for her. After an hour or so she was found walking down the road unaware of the search. The mysterious disappearance was never solved.

Bill King's final days on duty at Camp David weren't spent the way he wanted. But then President Johnson was on board. "I was hoping that during my last month at Camp David that we would have no visitors and it would be peaceful and quiet. Sure enough, it wasn't.

The President was unhappy with his cabin and he was there for three of the final weekends. "Sure enough, there were problems," King glumly reported. "The president was unhappy with his air conditioning. On Saturday morning while most of the camp was sleeping, the president wasn't. And he vented his anger everywhere. We were still scratching our heads from the previous night's discomfort. But then, like the usual problem solving, the trouble was identified. We realized that JFK and LBJ both took naps and liked the room pitch black. We had to put blackout curtains up behind the drapes to keep light out. We shimmied the carpet behind the drapes to keep the light out and we checked to

---

We realized that JFK and LBJ both took naps and liked the room pitch black. We had to put blackout curtains up behind the drapes to keep light out.

---

make sure there were no leaks. The A/C outlet was in the bedroom and the return duct was in the hall. The staff had made the
room so 'light' proof, it prevented the return air from leaving the
room. They were either light sleepers or preoccupied by the problems of the day. But they simply couldn't get any sleep with such
distractions the president told King.

The crew made repairs but no sooner had they left when they
were called back for the same difficulty. Now the president wanted to see King in his room. "I went in and LBJ was propped up
with documents spread out around him. In a gruff voice, he said
'Look at the thermostat, commander.' I then related what we had
to do to make the room totally sealed and we showed him how we
planned to fix it. 'What am I going to do tonight?' the President
said. I told him 'to sleep with the door open. President Johnson
thought for a moment and then said 'OK.' That was my last contact with LBJ."

> *A Disciples of Christ Church member, Johnson continued the
> practice of holding church services at the camp in cafeterias
> and some of the large lodges. He felt it important under the
> circumstances and at the same time, he felt it essential to
> bring in leading church pastors from time to time.*

Just as the president finished his discussion he turned back
to the business at hand; more troops for Vietnam and shoring up
domestic law enforcement to handle protests that were increasing
in virtually every state in the union. Meanwhile, the president was
advised to send 1,000 Marines and 2,500 82nd Airborne troops
to protect American citizens and interests in President Donald Ca-
bral's troubled Dominican Republic. The situation was important
enough that LBJ invited Rev. Billy Graham to lead the Sunday
prayer at the camp.

The Johnson sisters, Lucy and Lynda, entertained their young friends at the camp and took advantage of the facilities at Camp David while enjoying first run movies, bowling, swimming and skeet shooting. It had to be a fun time for two young ladies.

By the end of July, the President's advisers were regular visitors as Vietnam went from an irritating matter to a grave issue. Adviser Clark Clifford in his book Counsel to the President offered a glimpse of how the Catoctin retreat helped everyone relax during very stressful times. "At 5:45 p.m. on Sunday, President Johnson asked me to join Bob McNamara at Aspen Lodge. The

large, glassed –in living-dining-room looking out over a beautiful panorama view I could see through the large window to the right of the little golf course that Ike had installed and straight ahead, the lovely green hills called the Catoctin Mountains...Aspen was decorated as a hunting lodge with unassuming furnishings surrounding a large fireplace on one side. On the left side of the living room was a rectangular dining room table around which the President often held conferences and late night meetings." When they ended discussions, said Clifford, they returned to their cottages to wait word about dinner or going home. "While we waited, the president did something quite unusual. He drove around Camp David area alone for an hour; then for another hour he walked the ground, also alone." Clifford didn't forget that insight into the President's meditation.

What did he enjoy most while at the retreat? Movies, bowling, walking about the camp or simply sitting on the patio. On January 30, 1964 a trial balloon was floated to change the name from David back to Shangri-La. To his credit and in respect for the  camp's past, Johnson rejected a staff proposal. Some believe he did it out of respect for Eisenhower who, Johnson believed, had an attachment to the place and Roosevelt. In fact, Johnson let Ike know that he could use the camp any time. Records show that the Eisenhowers never asked for the keys nor used the place after they officially left.

Over the next few months, the president and his advisers got together at Camp David to discuss a nonproliferation treaty and the US intention to drop plans for a NATO nuclear fleet. In his book Vantage Point, the president said that following dinner "we reviewed our talks. Much of the time, we wandered over the paths and through the Autumn colored woods at Camp David."

Months later, the camp changed from a Naval Administrative Unit Annex to a Naval Support Facility. Why it wasn't called what it is, is still a mystery to me today. The world knows what it is and where it is. The subterfuge is thought to be a Navy thing.

In June, 1967, president and Mrs. Johnson were hosts to their first foreign leader, Prime Minister Harold Holt and Mrs. Holt of Australia for an unscheduled visit. The Holts were originally going to visit the Johnsons at the Johnson ranch in Texas. However, Soviet Premier Alexei Kosygin arrived in New York for a United Nations meeting and the president felt it was important enough to stay in Washington in case a meeting with the Soviet leader was arranged.

> Months later, the camp changed from a Naval Administrative Unit Annex to a Naval Support Facility. Why it wasn't called what it is....is still a mystery to me today. The world knows what it is and where it is.

The quick change in locations was nothing new to the Camp David staff but still posed the challenges of those who serve on call to decision makers. Aides credited the camp staff in helping to make the quickly arranged meeting a successful two-day visit.

The two couples surprised each other by showing home movies of their families on Saturday night, a first for Camp David visits. On Sunday morning both families and a party of 15 guests attended church services at the Harriet Chapel in Catoctin Furnace. Following the service, the Johnsons and Holts spent time chatting

with parishioners and watching the children play. That July, the president greeted Canadian Prime Minister Lester Pearson and the two men held a private meeting before holding a joint press conference on the lower patio of Aspen Lodge. According to Johnson aide Jack Valenti, the meeting became somewhat "frosty" when Pearson voiced opposition to US policies. But, said Valenti, the two western leaders "parted friends." "There is something about Camp David that makes you feel softer," Valenti told reporters.

According to Johnson aide Jack Valenti, the meeting became somewhat "frosty" when Pearson voiced opposition to US policies. But, said Valenti, the two western leaders "parted friends." "There is something about Camp David that makes you feel softer," Valenti told reporters.

In less than a year, Lyndon Johnson announced he would "not seek and I will not accept the nomination of my party as your President" for re-election. Shortly after his announcement, the president went to Camp David where he told senior advisers that he was seeking peace talks to end the Vietnam war. Those in attendance at Camp David were: Ambassador to Vietnam Ellsworth Bunker, defense secretary Clifford; Walt Rostow, chairman of the joint chiefs Earle G. Wheeler, MacGeorge Bundy and Averill Harriman and others. Discussion focused on the selection of a site for the meetings. For the first time a press office was established in Thurmont and all releases were to come from the Thurmont location.

Several weeks later, Johnson flew to Camp David to spend a few days. "It was a relief to get away from the noise and carbon monoxide of downtown Washington," he said in his memoirs.

"At the Aspen Lodge I changed into more comfortable clothes and sat in the living room talking with Walt Rostow about the problems we would face the next day. Finally I dozed off in my chair until dinnertime. We went to the Lodge and over breakfast, talked about Vietnam and the latest exchanges with Hanoi. We later moved outside to enjoy the sunshine and continue our discussions."

Camp David proved an excellent place to relax and explore others' thoughts. Said A Guided Tour of Camp David about John-son's attitude toward Camp David he came to find it  comfortable. Yet, when I was with him back in Ohio as one of a number of aides trying to keep up with his long strides on a "walk and talk" as we called it under our breath he said, as he had a number of times, that he preferred his ranch. I doubt that a Texan would enjoy the amount of snow dumped on Camp David at times.

He didn't.

by John "Jack" Behrens

Chapter 6
A Fall From Grace

For a young man from poor Quaker family, Richard Nixon's life was shaped by an anger that gave him an inner strength of conviction and at the same time it destroyed much of the legacy he had hoped so much he would leave for posterity. America's 37th president, like many of his predecessors, served as an officer in the Navy in World War II but saw no combat. He returned home not to put up a shingle as lawyer from the prestigious Duke University but to get elected to Congress in 1946. Four years later, he became a United States senator from California.

He was in the right place at the right time when WWII hero, Supreme Allied Commander, Gen Dwight Eisenhower ran for president on the Republican ticket in 1952. At 39, Nixon offered a good balance in age with the 60-year-old Eisenhower. However, Nixon encountered the first of major gaffs that pursued him

nixonfoundation.org

through his political career. When it was discovered that he may have accepted questionable contributions he was forced to make a nationally televised address of contrition called the "Checkers" speech. A speech about a cocker spaniel which Nixon tried to emotionally link with voters but which failed to because people saw it backfire, because it was too emotional.

He introduced American TV viewers to the potential of a race to the moon. Neal Armstrong and Edwin "Buzz" Aldrin Jr., American astronauts, sent back word that they had taken one small step... "one giant leap for mankind." America was back in

the space race and planning its next mission. In foreign affairs, Nixon engineered so-called "secret plans" to bring about an accord with North Vietnam to end the fighting in Southeast Asia. In other foreign affairs, Nixon brought advances that were equally impressive. He accelerated the secret talks to bring an accord with North Vietnam to some success, but the plan collapsed as American forces scrambled to leave, fleeing across rooftops in Saigon. His meetings with Leonid Brezhnev brought about limiting strategic nuclear weapons. He appeared to reverse his previous position on China from early 1972 when he opened the door to a country long closed to the western world. His one and a portion terms brought significant changes at Camp David. Said William Safire, former speechwriter to Nixon, "Camp David was transformed

Camp David was transformed from a rustic hideaway into a mountain mansion and nobody ever asked how much it would cost...

from a rustic hideaway into a mountain mansion and nobody ever asked how much it would cost, much less how it appear as an

example of an administration dedicated to serving taxpayers' dollars."

Thanks to Bill Gulley and Mary Ellen Reese, a book called Breaking Cover 1980 told the story of corruption and power that covered much of Nixon's second term.

Again, Safire detailed what took place in his book, Before the Fall: "Camp David is far from rustic. It is a beautiful home complete with pool, sauna and movie projection booth, most people would consider luxurious. Rustic it is not. The cabin where the writer stayed was rustic."

And, it was Nixon who further enlarged the presidential hideaway and created an aura that Camp David and the White House were synonymous as he hid from public view by remaining at the heavily guarded Maryland mountainside

retreat. as Watergate swirled around him. Security was increased as the threats on the White House, Camp David and the President continued. According to camp personnel, "Richard Nixon changed the complexion and tone at Camp David." At the same he wanted to assist what visitors were in the region. To aid people in getting around better, the golf cart paths, previously used for walking, were paved for better cart transport.

Because it was a classified site --- and still is---the Appropriations Committee headed by George Mahon wanted to know about the changes proposed. Congress resisted some of the Nixon proposals. The Navy found the funds but there was still the mystery of

why President Nixon wanted the change. The problem was that the president wanted a specific spot for the pool he sought. Both he and Haldeman refused to budge. "That's what the president

wants," Haldeman insisted. In addition to the expensive relocation to accommodate the pool, Nixon also wanted a larger meeting room for his cabinet meetings to be held at Camp David. It was decided to upgrade Laurel, a smaller cabin, for an additional $700,000. To spruce up the underground bomb shelter, which had an elevator right as you enter the main camp lodge, it would cost an additional $250,000 to enhance the bomb shelter itself. New bedspreads, new covers, new chairs, repainting the president's  offices and adding new paintings were also planned. I was never able to obtain the itemized cost for the upgrade of the president's office.

According to Julie Nixon Eisenhower, her mother and father weren't ostentatious about their love for one another, but she felt it was always there.

At the same time, she also felt that her parents enjoyed the freedom that Camp David offered. "My parents were freer at Camp David than anywhere else." she told media.

 Pat Nixon writing about the offices and rooms described the following in her explanation called Pat Nixon: The Untold Story: "Office hours followed modern presidents wherever they go. In Aspen Lodge, my father conferred with staff and visitors in a small study where mother had placed a replica of his favorite brown easy chair and ottoman which were covered in a blue silk."

What personnel were most likely there any time of the day or

He liked a swim and he liked a fire and the president of the United States could defy the seasons of the year to have them.

night? "Two Navy cooks and a
steward plus a military aide, the
camp commander and often the
White House photographer Ollie
Atkins routinely spent much of the
day in the kitchen," Pat reported in
her memoirs.

Safire recalls strange imagery
that followed him when he thought
about Nixon and nature on top of
the mountain. "First, that heated
swimming pool, sending up clouds
of vapor in the cool mountain air and a second, of that crackling
fire in the oval office during the hottest days of the summer with
the air conditioning turned up high. He liked a swim and he liked
a fire and the president of the United States could defy the seasons
of the year to have them." Like several other presidents, Ronald
Reagan for example, they were impressed with Hollywood's production and quality. Nixon, with his good golfing friend BeBe,
are estimated to have watched over 150 Hollywood films at the
White House's Family Theater and Camp David. The titles they
saw were among the film capital's best. They were impressed with
the movie Patton, musicals and the ultra-patriotic Yankee Doodle
Dandy with James Cagney. They enjoyed movies that portrayed
ugly characters in a way that helped viewers understand the good
guys from the bad. As simple as a number of those early movies
were the clarity of the righteous was visible in most and, like most
of us, Richard Nixon wanted us to believe there was virtue in his
life and purpose. "Life isn't meant to be easy. It's hard to take being on the top or on the bottom, I guess I'm something of a fatal-

*Life isn't meant to be easy. It's hard to take being on the top or
on the bottom, I guess I'm something of a fatalist. You have to
survive some of these things. Life is one crisis after another ...*

ist. You have to survive some of these things. Life is one crisis after another," he said to a commencement audience. Yet his stature as a leader in not surrendering to crowds was sustained in his defeat. In a speech during his presidency he gave us insight to his philosophy: "You must never be satisfied with losing. You must get angry, terribly angry about losing. But the mark of the good loser is that he takes his anger out on himself and not on his victorious opponent or his teammates," he explained.

Camp David served as his staging base to renew his battles. For some time, he seemed to feel he could conquer any enemy with words. The world finds Americans have a hard time with such failures of misunderstanding and interpretation. Our "can do" culture makes us believe moral right will always succeed. Richard Nixon was neither a success nor failure but you have to admire his stand on conviction. Camp David became his "home" away from home where he could, for example, direct his mythical or-

Make use of Camp David. You will need it. I may criticize your policies, but 'of one thing I can assure you; I shall never join in any criticism of you, expressed or implied for taking time off for relaxation.' There is nothing more important than a president be physically, mentally and emotionally in the best possible shape to confront the immensely difficult decisions he has to make.

chestra with his arms conducting it in front of large speakers facing empty space and listening for the "fat lady to sing." His use of the retreat included the First Family and Pat. According to White House records, he used Camp David as much as the previous five

presidents. In his first two years he equaled as much the total of visits of Camp David's first 27 years! At the same time, he was one of the early proponents of upgrading the 29-year facility and bringing changes like a heated swimming pool, a two-lane bowling alley and two renovated cabins with indoor bathrooms and water.

His advice to new presidents: "Make use of Camp David. You will need it. I may criticize your policies, but 'of one thing I can assure you; I shall never join in any criticism of you, expressed or implied for taking time off for relaxation.' There is nothing more important than a president be physically, mentally and emotionally in the best possible shape to confront the immensely difficult decisions he has to make."

He probably would not have approved of the spoof of Camp David Christmas that appeared after his death on the whitehouse.gov website. The spoof mocks the secrecy surrounding and offers this holiday solution: "In the holiday spirit of openness, and transparency, President Obama is pleased to offer the American People this year to experience a traditional Camp David Christmas. Invited guests will arrive at noon on Christmas Eve and

stay for three nights in one of the ten cabins. An average cabin comes equipped with two bedrooms and a small living room with a fireplace. A traditional Christmas Eve dinner will be served inside Laurel Lodge. After dinner, gather around a Christmas tree and exchange presents with loved ones. Then enjoy some steaming hot chocolate and not forget to hang the stockings. Take horse drawn sleigh ride around the retreat to view the Christmas scene with a visit to Evergreen Chapel which will host midnight Christmas Eve candlelight service. For the first time ever, the Domestic Surveillance Directorate will grant the White House access to their reference and extrapolate a list of the best citizen candidates to invite for this holiday experience. We know because they know. And now you know too. Have a nice holiday."

Who says that Washington doesn't enjoy the humor in its work!

by John "Jack" Behrens

Chapter 7
A Man For All Seasons

When Gerald Ford took the oath of office for his one term as president, Aug. 9, 1974, he told the American people how extraordinary his role had become. He wasn't bragging or overstating when he said: "I assume the presidency under extraordinary circumstances ... this is an hour of history that troubles our mind and hurts our hearts."

He was speaking from the heart when he told reporters of his decision. He encountered fateful choices not once but twice in less than a year. He was a popular Michigan congressman during his 25 years in the US House of Representatives well known for his integrity and openness at a time when both were in critical short supply in Washington. He described himself as a "moderate on domestic issues, a conservative in fiscal affairs" and "a dyed in the wool internationalist" where other topics were concerned. I met him once at a political rally where I had to shout my question over

the din of a boisterous crowd. He gave me a brief comment concerning the launching of Sputnik weeks before his press conference but more importantly, he gave me his assessment of the man who would become president in a few years. Ford and Jack Kennedy were close to one another in the Old Capitol Office Building and became friends on the basis of their chats to and from the House chambers. "I find him smart, an honorable man, decent and frankly I liked Jack from the start although I didn't agree with his philosophy," said Ford.

The Michigan legislator was clearly the choice of congressional leaders when bribery charges against Spiro Agnew forced him to step down as vice president in December, 1973. Ironically, it was Gerald Ford, a National Honor Society, Varsity Letter athlete at Grand Rapids High School, who helped pass the 25th Amendment which, years earlier, prescribed the procedure for selecting Vice Presidential candidates. Eight months later, fate intervened once more when Gerald Rudolf Ford, then Republican Minority Leader, was sworn in as President of the United States to replace the deposed Richard Nixon whose sudden resignation Aug. 8,

1974, brought shock to the nation and the world. Given the urgency of the request he had little time to ponder his decision. The public viewed his response as what was needed during such a crisis.

The Ford family did relax at the Maryland retreat and it relished the sports equipment and fields of play available to them. The family loved golf and tennis on clay courts where they competed with friends and guests as well as staff. Of all those who participated in athletics at the camp, the president worked the hardest to stay in shape. Most who got to know him found that his demeanor and consistency were his

mental guides whether it was athletics or conversation. Though it was more than likely the Secret Service who took snowmobiles to Camp David first, it was the Ford family who were first seen using the winter snow machines in and around the triple fenced wall that separates the camp from the rest of Frederick County, MD. While locals say that

snowmobiling is a great sport in the area, most say they would advise outsiders and visitors to go cautiously. "It's rugged country and no place for a person who doesn't know the terrain or their vehicle," said one former Maryland native.

Jerry Ford, accompanied by First Lady Betty, Steven, Susan and two young family friends Gardner Britt and DeeDee Jarvis made their first visit to upstate Maryland in the early fall days of August,

1974. Staff said they were like a typical family with teens turned loose on Disney World. They tried everything. They swam, tried their hands at skeet, went horseback riding and still found hours left in the day for golf on Ike's four-hole course. Later in the year, the family—primarily the president and Susan---thoroughly enjoyed showing natives they too were no amateurs on the snowmobile trails. Growing up in Michigan certainly prepared them for bone-jarring cold temperatures. The president got involved in the outings too, when he could. He documented, for example, the family's first visit to Aspen Lodge. They were accompanied on this trip by television commentator, Harry Reasoner of ABC. The president's openness probably produced an unexpected result, too. The media and the president became more willing to listen to one another, an important development that came from Ford's tenure. And he, also, found it necessary to make sure that people, reporters and others knew how he viewed people on the national stage. About Lyndon Johnson, for example, Ford explained that when Johnson and he served on a joint committee to examine the Sputnik threat, Johnson "appointed himself chairman."

Nixon's foul moods and disposition as well as his salty language caused media people to name his cabin "Poison Ivy Lodge." Ford brought such a change in attitudes in a short time that the name was changed. "It became so friendly that a new sign was prepared and labeled "Honeysuckle, to demonstrate the change," one observer said. It was introduced at the lodge by Reasoner and 24 journalists who had joined the impromptu protest for change. One reason for media annoyance with conditions at Camp David during the Ford Administration was that the

president's lodge was so situated it couldn't be observed from some press locations. For example, even a powerful telescope couldn't get a view of the activities at the president's quarters. Making matters worse, of course, no helicopters were permitted.

"A few civilians such as landscape gardeners and some pool caretakers visit but under tight security. The Navy Seabees who compose the vast majority of the military personnel assigned to the retreat guard the cabins and sports facilities and service the highly sophisticated communications system." said author Peter Michelmore in his book Camp David: Hideaway for Presidents.

To add to its arsenal of emergency vehicles, the Secret Service purchased several snowmobiles during the Carter Administration to transport the president and family from a remote area where several or more feet of snow could pose a challenge for a four-wheel vehicle.

Another change that outsiders weren't aware of was the perk Ford quietly gave senior White House staff and cabinet members. Certain staff and cabinet members were allowed to use the facility when the president and first lady weren't on the premises. Most of those I talked with said the cooperation between media and government was improved dramatically during Ford's brief tenure. A number of meetings were held during the period too. The Office of Management and Budget Conference met in October, followed by the Energy Conferences of December, 1974; these meetings along with a Presidential Clemency Board, European Economic

Community Conference in 1975, Europe Economic Community Conference in January 1976. The president and Mrs. Ford hosted one foreign head of state who called while enroute to Japan. President and Mrs. Suharto of Indonesia made the visit on their way. Some suggested that such use showed the retreat wasn't unused. It could have been making some income too, although such reports were rare.

The first lady, meantime, was subjected to her own difficulties early when she tried to raise her family. of three kids in a two bedroom apartment. She finally confronted her husband and he agreed the problem had to be resolved. It was...that night!

Meanwhile, at Camp David the battle over which air service would transport the president and his guests continued. Presidential aides asked the Marines to investigate the front lawn of the White House as a landing site. The car caravans were becoming more an irritation to DC drivers mired in more traffic each year. It seemed obvious to some that the Marines had won the right. Later it was determined that there were safety issues. The Army's choppers, VH-3, were aging and a replacement had to be sought. In the interim, Lockheed Martin's VH-71 was chosen but within months it was rejected. The Navy called for more discussion, it was left undecided and the Army used the call sign Army One when the president was aboard. In 1975, Marine One flew the missions with an all-female crew for the first time.

During the first visit of 1975, the president spent time talking with crew members in the mess hall, barracks and club and he and the First Lady continued the practice of attending church services  in surrounding communities. The Fords attended Easter Services at the Catoctin Episcopal Parish, Harriet Chapel, Catoctin Furnace, August 18, 1976.

Betty Ford remembered the hours spent recounting the costs that had to be accounted for with dignitaries who came on board. According to the informal rules accepted as common practice at Camp David, the federal government paid for those considered official guests of the US government. Family costs had to be paid by family. But who paid for the Baked Alaska crab that was flown in from Fairbanks could be a mystery for days and sometimes never resolved. The chefs tried to accommodate the president and guests on exotic requests which lead to additional costs. "Once  a month we'd write a check for what we spent at Camp David," Ms. Ford said.

Betty offered a poignant note concerning the meaningful and magnificent last visit with the crew on Thanksgiving 1976. The First Family, accompanied by a small group of the personal friends made their final visit a warm and memorable occasion January 15.

by John "Jack" Behrens

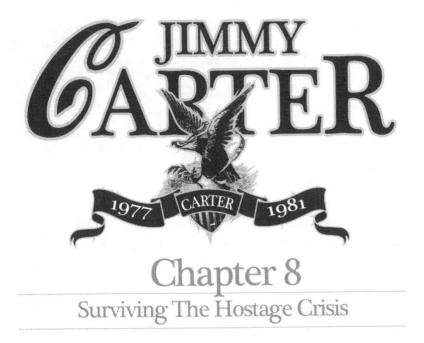

Chapter 8
Surviving The Hostage Crisis

President Jimmy Carter's account, Keeping Faith: Memoirs of a President, describes the painful difficulties American legislators and diplomats have encountered when trying to find peaceful solutions to centuries-old disagreements between Israel and her neighbors.

Carter seemed the ideal man for the presidency given his strong feelings about human rights and his resolve to end the suffering among Jews, Palestinians and Arabs.

But, like most American politicians who become President, the foreign and domestic tasks are too numerous, and each takes time to sort out and digest before anything can be done. And, a shrill demand for answers now added pressure on the elected. Carter, for example, faced more domestic problems than anticipated. Rising energy prices and unemployment were pressing issues, and on top of that, came establishing a national energy policy, tackling the complex Strategic Arms Limitation Talks (SALT II) and facing a backlash from the public regarding the decision to return the Panama Canal Zone to Panama.

Carter's plate was overflowing when the Iranian students forced their way into the American Embassy and took 52 Americans hostage and held them until Jan. 20, 1981, the day Ronald Reagan became president. The American government, led by Carter, organized 13 days of secret talks involving Egyptian President Anwar Sadat and Israeli Prime Minister Menachem Begin. On Sept. 17, 1978, a two-point agreement which would address (1) the West Bank and Gaza and (2) would look at the Sinai.

The reaction to the proposal in the Arab World was very negative and, in a short time, there was an emergency meeting of the Arab League in November 1978, to discuss it. Carter admitted he was doubtful as "there are still a great number of difficulties that remain and many hard issues to be settled." Sadat's wife, Jehan, recalled that she encouraged him to keep negotiating with Begin. "You understand him, Anwar," she said. "You must keep trying." "I am trying and trying," Sadat added.

Of the three principals in the talks at Camp David, none could escape blame. Carter scored points for trying to bring the parties together and weathering the temperaments of the two leaders.

The Egyptian leader, who was Carter's first foreign guest at Camp David, continued to be concerned about US arms sales in the Middle East. In comments to American officials at Camp David, Sadat said that he had nothing against the "special relationship between the US and Israel." He said he was simply asking

for the same arms that Israel gets. "I have my own chosen fate and there is no way to turn back on this. I couldn't disappoint those millions of people who lived with us those moments in Jerusalem."

The Carters made their first visit to the camp about a month after inauguration in keeping with the tradition of his predecessors. The weekend of February 25, 1977, the president, First Lady Rosalynn, Chip and Caron Carter, Jeff and Annette Carter and daughter, Amy, took the Marine helicopter to one of the most isolated government retreats in the Western Hemisphere, Camp David.

Although a former Navy officer in the submarine service, Carter had to make hard decisions on planes, not ships, when meeting with Sadat. The Egyptian leader was looking to the United States to sell Egypt up to 120 F5E fighters to replace deteriorating Soviet aircraft. Parts were becoming hard to acquire and Sadat's advisers were urging the American government to help them retain a balance of power. The planes the Russian gave the Egyptians "were falling apart," American officials said.

Carter smiled when he was piped aboard in Navy tradition. The military personnel at Camp David from the first day were Navy, Marine and Seabee and nothing has changed. And, he made sure the whole family joined him

for the occasion. The crew at the camp noted that it was another vibrant young family, similar to the Kennedys and Fords. They loved the outdoors and the resources the retreat provided. When the Fords and Carters met at the White House on Inaugural Day, January 20, 1977, Rosalynn Carter said the conversation wasn't about linen, menus or the location of the bathrooms. The couples talked "...mostly about Camp David where the Fords had spent their last weekend. The food is so delicious there, Mrs. Ford tells, that she is going to have to go on a diet."

The Carters, like others, enjoyed swimming in the Aspen pool, bowling in the two-lane alley at Hickory Lodge, watching movies and exploring their new home away from home. President Carter summed it up later: "Camp David is truly beautiful, with cottages (all named after trees) and paths snuggled on top and down one side of a small mountain and by a thick growth of stately oak, poplar, ash, locust, hickory, and maple trees."

On this Fourth of July weekend, the president and the immediate Carter family had Miss Lillian up to celebrate the holiday. The

president had already taken steps to make sure that church services could be conducted while he was "on board." And Jimmy Carter never forgot to spend time at the camp carpentry shop or check conditions for fly fishing among the old-timers. One veteran fisherman said that he saw the glimmer in Carter's eyes as he talked about fishing.

The president continued the informal tradition of his predecessors by inviting senior staff members and their families to accompany him to the camp. There was, at the same time, some nervous talk about the forthcoming meeting with Sadat.

A deeply religious man, Carter asked that arrangements be made to conduct services during his Camp David visits. His predecessors had to improvise

church services because there was no formal chapel, although cabins were designated to be used as worship sites. On July 3, 1977, the theater in Hickory Lodge was easily converted into a chapel. The post chaplain at nearby Fort Richie, MD, provided a military field altar and hymnals and frequently he conducted the services. Each Sunday, an Army chaplain would conduct services for the president, his staff and members of the crew and what guests were on board at the time. When President Sadat of Egypt arrived in September 1978, he made a special request camp personnel hadn't heard before: President Sadat wanted a special place for the Egyptians to hold their religious service. Said Carter, "We set aside the room in Hickory Lodge where we always had church services when our family was at Camp David."

Typically, what was done for one participant was offered to the other and the theater in Hickory Lodge was made available to the Jewish delegation aboard. A Jewish religious holiday occurred during the summit ceremonies so, on Thanksgiving Day, 1980, the helicopter hanger was set up for church services and an army chaplain and the US Army Chorus of Washington, DC, made it a commemorative event. After the service, the president and Mrs. Carter enjoyed themselves greeting visitors and helping worshipers.

Since golf carts are the vehicle of choice, accidents were thought to be limited. The 11-year-old daughter of President Carter's National Security Adviser, Zbigniew Brzezinski, Mika, bumped the cart of Israeli leader, Menachem Begin. There were no injuries, just loads of embarrassed people and a media "making much ado about nothing," said a security officer as the story went worldwide. Amy Carter wasn't driving the cart at the time.

The Carters felt that since they were at mid-term in Jimmy's presidency it was time to reassess the Carter presidency. "Rosalynn and I decided before I called the staff together that we would stay at Camp David for a few days and have some people come in whom we trusted to give me advice on where we should go from here," the president told the staff later.

Meanwhile, President Carter used the interim to determine if peace negotiations could be achieved. He conducted a domestic summit by inviting a variety of experienced people to join him at

the camp. Before it ended, more than 130 prominent American leaders were meeting with the president at the Catoctin site and expressing their opinions. They ranged from members of Congress, corporation and business leaders, union heads, economists, energy experts, political advisers and veteran news columnists and reporters.

"It (Camp David) had not been designed to accommodate so many people, especially when they came from three different nations and represented three distinct cultures. Sadat, Begin and I had private cabins within a stone's throw of each other. None of the other cottages were more than a few hundred yards from us and all of them were packed to the limit with people," Carter said.

As the days passed, the two delegations found "the close proximity of the living quarters engendered an atmosphere of both isolation and intimacy conducive to easing the tension and encouraging informality," Carter noted.

As the days passed, the two delegations found "the close proximity of the living quarters engendered an atmosphere of both isolation and intimacy conducive to easing the tension and encouraging informality," Carter noted.

The last time the Camp David crew had faced such demands, veterans said, was the visit of Leonid Brezhnev in 1973. This time they had a good feeling about how they

had supported the commander-in-chief and become the strength of the mission. It all came together on Feb. 3, 1978, when President and Mrs. Sadat joined President and Mrs. Carter for the 35 minute trip from the White House to Camp David in Marine One, the presidential helicopter. Secretary of State Vance had offered personal invitations to President Sadat and Prime Minister Begin in July and both "accepted enthusiastically." Many meetings had taken place at Aspen (the president's lodge) and Holly

and crew members congratulated themselves for creating the atmosphere to make it an event to remember. The three heads of state were able to leave for Washington on September 17, to jointly sign the Camp David Accords, confident of their goals. In February 1979, Secretary of State Vance, Prime Minister Khalil of Egypt, Foreign Minister Dayan of Israel and their staffs, met at Camp David again to continue the Middle East talks in an atmosphere very different from the more contentious early gatherings. Said Carter later, "the demands on the communications crew during the 13 historic days were significant in keeping the faith."

The highs and lows of the Carter presidency, some insist, came from events that he had no control or influence over. Others believe Carter failed to use all the diplomatic tools in restoring the US respect at home and abroad. Said a government report during the bleak holiday season 1979, "the hostage situation, which would trouble him throughout the remainder of his administration, was particularly painful for the president. He had vowed not

to light the great Christmas tree just south of the White House to signify the nation's sorrow over the hostages' loss of freedom." Refraining from a normal social life, the president, First Lady and Amy spent a quiet and lonely Christmas. In March 1979, in a simple ceremony, Sadat and Begin signed the right to self-determination agreement on the last day of the agreement. It formally ended the war between the two nations.

The world praised the two leaders for bringing about the settlement. The Nobel Peace Prize was awarded to both nations for their resolve. Carter was praised for using his influence and office to bring concessions. It brought about a hard fought victory over prejudice. Egypt agreed to diplomatically recognize the state of Israel and give Israeli ships access to the Suez. With all the phrase editing and diplomacy, the treaty once again didn't solve the problem.

While Carter's critics were many, others found him to be passionate about issues he espoused. For example, he negotiated the impossible when he brought Israel and Egypt together to sign and agree to the Camp David Accords. Earlier, he helped negotiate the Panama Canal Treaty. But, the success with the treaty was followed by another dark cloud that appeared when major personnel changes had to be made and embarrassing details smeared the administration.

Controversy had begun in the early days when a few of the president's closest friends were charged with accusations of corruption and violations of federal statutes. Bert Lance, Director of the Carter Office of Management and Budget, resigned from his position under pressure while he was chairman of the board of Calhoun National Bank. He was cleared of charges but harmed Carter's effort in a celebrated trial in 1981. Add to that Carter's ill-advised political decision to pardon virtually all Vietnam draft evaders and his lifting of the threat of prosecution for those who left the country. The stigma of corruption was minor compared to Carter's heavy handed role in promoting Middle East peace, some said.

When President Carter convened his cabinet for a complete reassessment and found more hostility to his decisions, Time magazine observed: "In the whole history of American politics, there had never been anything quite like it."

The Christmas of '79 was one of the more joyless holidays at Camp David. The reason, of course, was the Iranian hostage crisis. The president, in keeping with his own statement, refused to light the national Christmas tree on the South Lawn of the White

House. Instead, he went to Camp David where he and his family kept to themselves. They played tennis, swam in the Aspen pool, jogged and played in a crew-softball game. Movies continued to  be important to relieve the pressure of the issues he faced. The family spent hours at Camp David relaxing with Hollywood's best PG entertainment.

 His support came from followers like Ronald Reagan who sent this email message: "Jimmy Carter has been ridiculed, lambasted and condemned by his critics, and this post is not an attempt to deny the weaknesses and mistakes of his presidency. Carter has learned how to accept the reality that he is shown little respect for his virtues and accomplishments with a lot of it due to his defeat for reelection in 1980 by the charismatic Ronald Reagan, who is often now seen as a deity in many circles. There is the reality that if a president loses reelection, his reputation in history suffers dramatically, no matter what he had achieved in office."

As the days passed, the two delegations found "the close proximity of the living quarters engendered an atmosphere of both isolation and intimacy conducive to easing the tension and encouraging informality," Carter noted.

by John "Jack" Behrens

RONALD REAGAN

1981 · REAGAN · 1989

Chapter 9

He Made Americans Feel Good Again

He took office on one of the coldest days of January, 1981. His election the previous November as the 40th President of the United States had brought the release of 52 American hostages from the American Embassy in Iran. His predecessor, Jimmy Carter, warned he wouldn't ok any deal until the hostages were back on U.S. soil. Both presidents were successful, although polls show the American people were solidly behind the actor and G.E. host, Ronald Reagan, to steer the country.

President Reagan, who spent his college days broadcasting his alma mater's games, flirted with a career in broadcast journalism, but graduated from Eureka College in 1932 with a degree in economics. He might have become another Walter Cronkite, Chet Huntley or David Brinkley.

CHAPTER 9

He loved to work behind the microphone and spent considerable time going back and forth to Chicago trying to find any broadcast spot he could get. A seasoned manager told him one day that he'd do better just getting "a job." He put his college experience to work and the American people rewarded his work ethic. He was a natural in front of the camera and in the broadcast studio. No doubt, he could have had his own radio or television show in the 1970's and 80's.

His strength, according to opponents and friends alike, was his ability to tell a story. He knew how to tell "a great story," all agreed. He knew when to create laughter and when to pause. "And he didn't overstep the pause that audiences need to make the point," said a commencement speaker, not long ago. What most of his audiences didn't know, is that although he wore contact lenses, he would remove one lens to see his audience and leave the other to read his speech. His "double vision" caused him to get hit often while playing sports.

A veteran Hollywood actor, president of the Actors Guild and a spokesman for the General Electric Co., Reagan made the move from actor to politician when he took his special skills to the Republican Party in 1981 and became a political leader, too.

To some, he was one of the great presidents, while others held him in contempt as a rank amateur who knew how to "work a crowd, but nothing else." Two things we do know about his presidency are: (1.) He visited Camp David more than all the presidents before him --- traveling 187 times for a total of 571 days, and (2.) He and second wife, Nancy, according to White House records, saw 365 Hollywood films from 1981 until 1989 at the retreat.

Starting in March, 1981, the president and Mrs. Reagan visited Camp David and would, from time to time, bring along some senior advisers, family members or they merely went alone. The Reagans were delighted at the opportunity to enjoy solitary strolls on the campus or the wooded trails at the retreat. They frequently continued their discussions on horseback, riding the trails that had been laid out for the Kennedy family years earlier.

The couple brought in evening entertainment to the patios of the camp like country and western singer Janie Fricke and the Navy group, Country Currents, on the Aspen patio for a "down home" Texas barbecue. Of course, there were wholesome movies to watch too. The Reagans weren't the first horse people at Camp David, though; Dwight Eisenhower was, as were Lyndon Johnson and the Kennedys.

The president used the novelty of the mountain retreat to bring in people from the "hill" (Congress) for political events and old-fashioned rallies on government property! On July 26, 1981, 13 members of Congress were guests of the president for a casual luncheon and a chance to see the real Camp David. I found it astonishing though, that so many members of Congress had not been to Camp David at all. But, occasional visits by powerful people like Justice and Mrs. Potter Stewart and their family, helped when the president was hosting foreign dignitaries and conducting meetings of importance.

The Reagans continued the education of Congress about Camp David in July when 13 more members of Congress were invited to the retreat for a casual luncheon and a tour of the facility. Again, in August, 38 Congress persons were given a Reagan tour of the camp along with lunch.

In June, 1981, the president entertained President Lopez-Portillo of Mexico for several days of working meetings. To many who witnessed the event, it was clear the gallery was more impressed by their horsemanship than their governing skills. The crowd also admired First Lady Nancy Reagan's beautiful array of radiant garden colors. The riding skill both men displayed brought applause from the staff members who appreciated the finer techniques of riding. Crew members remembered days when they were treated to fine displays of leisurely riding.

The Reagans arrived in Washington at the same time as the VCR was introduced, but they declined to use it. They preferred to show films by a projector with an operator. The first film was a secretary's story called, Working Girl, with Dolly Parton. While their final screen story at the camp from the old days was a Western called, Cattle Queen of Montana, it was shot in 1954 with Hollywood starlet, Barbara Stanwyck and Jack Elam and provided the typical western that Reagan starred in during his career. On his 77th birthday, the Reagans watched a movie he starred in early in his career, The Santa Fe Trail, the fictionalized story of George Custer and his exploits.

Sometimes, his movie selections were prompted by issues he faced. The night before he unveiled his proposal for a nuclear arms treaty with the Soviets, he watched the movie War Games, a film that features a teenager who intercepts North American Air Defense Command computers and nearly ignites World War III. Contrary to gossip, he enjoyed showing his guests a film that caused him some embarrassment at one time. In the movie, Bedtime with Bonzo, he was cast with a real chimp and he told his Camp David guests about the hazards of making a movie with a chimp. At the same time, his emotions and opinions became clear to many while he watched a title called Kiss of the Spider Woman. It was the story of the life and death of homosexuals and a left wing radical who they met in a South American jail. He became so upset that he ordered the movie turned off before it ended. The Reagans couldn't understand why aide Michael Deaver recommended it. The question was never answered in public, but the film wasn't shown again.

A strong conservative and anti-communist who had argued against such threats while president of the Actors' Guild, he obviously separated his political views from movie making years later when he watched Dolly Parton and Henry Fonda's daughter, Jane, work together in the movie, Working Girl.

Nancy and staff got together for lunch and a tour of the retreat. The invited guests enjoyed the opportunity to meet the president and Mrs. Reagan. But, the Reagans did decide to return to California in August, as they had done each of their eight years in the White House.

The president and Mrs. Reagan didn't forget the people at the camp who made their Washington stay enjoyable either. Nancy Reagan, for example, took the time to create a cost cutting blend of furniture in the guest cabins. They had not been upgraded since the 1970's. And, they had fun, too. After their last visit in 1989, the Reagans had lunch with the crew in the camp galley and a Christmas photo was taken.

Those who were invited to White House events were impressed with her efforts, considering the financial restraints at the time. Just before Christmas 1982, the president and first lady met with the camp's Hick-ory Theater crew to send out Christmas and holiday greetings and express their apprecia-tion for what had been done. Photos were tak-en and a one-time event celebration became an annual observance.

Starting on Sept 11, 1982, the president's familiarity and suc-cess with radio broadcasts created regular programming at the camp. To keep the American public well aware of topical issues featuring such subjects as the Lebanon situation, crime and crimi-nal justice, criminal justice reform and international free trade, were broadcast from 1982, First Lady Nancy Reagan joined the president for a joint broadcast about federal drug policy. It gave her the chance to discuss the federal policy and the platform to express her strong feelings about the human tragedies involved with the use of illicit drugs. She used the moment to talk of her efforts to launch a concerted national drive against drugs.

She received critical acclaim from throughout the free world. The Reagans spent their remaining free time in the year formulating plans to continue the drive against illicit drugs and supporting the president's drug policy.

The president, meanwhile, used his time at the camp working on a number of major addresses, including his State of the Union talk and his 1984 acceptance speech.

The Reagans met with the camp crew at the Hickory Theater and members of the crew and the President and First Lady posed for photographs. After a lunch served in the crew's galley the president talked about the situations in Lebanon and Grenada. The First Couple and the crew had lunch in the galley a number of times during their eight years.

The president showed his thanks and respect for the British government when he hosted Prime Minister Margaret Thatcher of Great Britain just before Christmas 1984 at Camp David. It was a warm, friendly meeting, which staff members said was very relaxed and the president enjoyed

offering a tour of Camp David to the prime minister, pointing out places of interest, such as where President Roosevelt and Prime Minister Churchill had met in the Holly Lodge during the war. As Mrs. Thatcher prepared to return to Great Britain, it was apparent that she enjoyed her visit. The Reagans and the prime minister took time to reflect and talk of their respect for one another. Prime Minister Margaret Thatcher of Great Britain became the only head of state to visit Camp David twice during the Reagan tenure in the White House.

While several presidents informally let staff and cabinet members use the camp when they weren't at the mountain, Reagan did not. But, he did make an exception for White House counselor Ed Meese. "Even Ronnie's closest advisers were rarely there," Nancy once said. Meese and his wife were invited to use Camp David in the summer of 1982 shortly after the death of their son in a car accident, so that they could get "their lives back together."

Another visitor who spent time at Camp David was the Japanese Prime Minister Nakasone, who visited the camp in April, 1986. The two leaders exchanged gifts in Aspen Lodge. The prime minister was given a traditional Camp David windbreaker. Windbreakers were given to most invited guests at Camp David.

The Reagan's final visit with the crew was a highly emotional stop. Most presidents and their spouses who used the camp facilities became attached to staff, but the bond was that much stronger for the Reagans. "We saw them frequently when they came aboard and

they were always very friendly.
It lifted your day, actually, "one
crew member who had been on
board for all their visits, told me.

The Reagan's final days
aboard were like their first,
Nancy said. "It was a very
cold and icy weekend, but we
wanted this time to say special
goodbye." A special farewell
was given to the First Family in
the hanger just before its final
departure. The entire Navy and
Marine Corps crew, in addition
to the Camp David detachment
of the White House Communications Agency, along with personnel from the Catoctin Mountain Park, attended. There were few
dry eyes when each group presented the couple with special me-
mentos of their time at Camp David. Referring to what he called
the "Good Ship Camp David," "of all the things we've done in
this presidency, we will miss Camp David the most!" His eyes
teared as he said the words.

When they left the camp, Ron and Nancy Reagan had spent
571 days at Camp David...more than any other president and
First Lady, at that time.

Just 69 days after he was sworn to uphold the Constitution as
president, Reagan was shot while leaving the Washington Hilton by
John Hinckley Jr. a deranged stalker of actress, Jodie Foster. Hinckley
was convinced, he told police later, that he would become a national
celebrity for such an act. It wasn't his first attempt to assassinate: he
tried to kill Jimmy Carter and got to within a foot of Carter in Nash-
ville before he was stopped. In the weeks that followed Hinckley
wrote notes to Foster who promptly turned them over to the police.

During his first year in office, Reagan spent more time horseback riding at Camp David than anything else. Reagan admitted that the shooting haunted him years later. Prior to the shooting, president and Mrs. Reagan reported complaining about the large number of Secret Service personnel assigned to them.

The ranch had been purchased in 1974 largely because of its remoteness. It was used mainly as a retreat where they could escape the telephone and cameras...

They said a sizable number of agents traveled with them to their 880 acre ranch in California, 20 miles from Santa Barbara and the agents were spoiling their seclusion. The president was particularly perturbed by agents who hovered over them when they took their daily horseback rides. The ranch had been purchased in 1974 largely because of its remoteness. It was used mainly as a retreat where they could escape the telephone and cameras, and work with his two exercises, horseback riding and chopping wood without interference.

The attempt on the president's life, his speedy recovery, and his smile while he rebuilt his strength, rallied the American people. His approval ratings were consistently in the 70's. He believed that God had spared him so he could fulfill a greater purpose. One of the Secret Service agents assigned to his detail left federal employment to become a pastor. He returned to the White House on April 25, a month after the shooting, and typical of Reagan, he was quite humble amidst the cheers and applause.

He received a standing ovation from the crowd in the White House and he responded by telling them "I should be applauding you." What was the cost of the Reagan Camp David during that period? Actual budget figures are very difficult to find. Don't forget the wars and rumors of wars that the United States engaged in between 1945 and 1960. The figures I obtained from the budget office were tightly held by the White House Military Office and the Department of the Navy. The Navy had been involved with Camp David (then Shangri-La) since its beginning with FDR. It continues today. By the end of 1981, the cost of operations and maintenance had increased to $1,140,000. By the end of 1982, the costs were $27,000 higher and growing, and analysts were fearful that there was "no safe landing."

"The whole purpose of going to the ranch was to be where he could work by himself, rather than business as usual," Meese told reporters. "If you want to have business, you stay at the White House or go to Camp David." Meese said that Reagan didn't want the ranch becoming a large operation carrying the title, "Western White House."

Such factors influenced Mr. Reagan to decide he and Nancy could be better protected and retain privacy at Camp David, rather than the California home.

by John "Jack" Behrens

GEORGE HW BUSH

1989   BUSH   1993

Chapter 10

Found interest, competition in a sport called Wallyball

President George HW Bush, 41 made his name in a sport that was coming East and gaining in popularity every season as a fun sport to watch. The sport was Wallyball, a combination racquetball, tennis and volleyball played under a different banner. Camp David was one of the few military bases that had the game.

George was a natural athlete who captained the baseball team at Yale after play on Andover Prep teams in soccer and baseball. According to his instructors, he was one of those bright achievers who excelled at virtually everything he tried. He was voted third most popular in the graduating class of 1942.

According to his instructors he was one of those bright achievers who excelled at virtually everything he tried.

He was patriotic, headstrong and by June 1943, he was an Ensign in the Navy, headed for flight school, against his parents' wishes. As the youngest pilot in the Navy, he flew the TBF avenger bomber named after his girlfriend Barbara Pierce, 16 a relative of President Benjamin Pierce.

The young bomber pilot also learned how to conduct aerial reconnaissance photography and taught others the skill of taking photos during combat. As an aerial combat reconnaissance photographer trainee, I used the training manuals that Bush prepared and flew in a single engines L–19 Piper Cubs to film strip the coasts of the United States a task that had been overlooked after World War II.

He left the service after his discharge. He attended Yale and continued to show his motivation to achieve. A first baseman on the Yale baseball team, the club won the Eastern Regional Championship two years in a row. The team played in the first ever college World Series in 1947. In the classroom he continued to have great interest in gathering more information about historical subjects and the world in general. A voracious historical nonfiction reader, he read 14 Lincoln biographies

during the last three years of his presidency and another 186 books ranging from Gore Vidal to Willa Cather.

In 1951 as the country entered a police action that became a war in Korea, George got together with a friend and formed an independent oil company. He entered politics in the 1960s and won a decisive victory in the Iowa caucuses. By 1980 George Bush was being considered for the presidency. He served as vice president to Pres. Ronald Reagan and had a glimpse of the oval office for eight years. When Reagan was shot in 1985, he went in for surgery and the black box which accompanies the Commander in Chief at all

times was transferred to the Bush staff. George and Barbara noted as they ended their turn at Vice Presidency that they had lived in the Vice President's mansion longer than any other residents since they were married 40 years before. It was a milestone in a public service career that included various assignments such as a tour as CIA director.

Bush was chosen by the American people as president in 1988 but he wasn't given a mandate.

Camp David recreation sites were numerous after Richard Nixon's tenure. Dwight Eisenhower had introduced a clever short one whole equals three golf game, close to the Aspen Lodge. Tennis courts, swimming pools, including a heated one, were added.

The president and Chris Evert played a doubles match at the camp in 1990 and raised $1.2 million for charity during the day. She talked about the significance of the match at her 1995 Tennis Hall of Fame induction ceremony. "We were at Camp David when the Gulf war broke out. He was working hard on the phone and came out and said 'I need a break. Let's play a set.'"

The Bush family added Wallyball as the 1980s began. The family was led by George HW, a veteran player who was followed by his son, George W. George Senior was considered one of the outstanding Wallyball players in the country. The game was imported to Camp David for military personnel and a

good number participated. Wallyball began in California and moved east quickly because of its popularity. It was started to help racquetball court owners get the use of their investment. Here's what a Wallyball player

said about the matches and the competitors at Camp David on the eve of the 2000 presidential election: "Whenever Bush played, he only wanted to play with family or crew. I was taught to play by two Bush team members. Neither one is here now. Tournaments were routinely held to see who had the skill. Both George Sr. and George W. had the physical size to make the saves and spikes that the game demanded. With secrecy shroud-

ing the base, unlike other installations, not many got to see some of the contests. George W and George H usually played together. If not they hand-picked their teams. As the president was quite good he wanted to play with competitive players. Oddly, they always picked four top players to play against. The goal of every Camp David player, I can tell you, was to spike on the President of the United States it happened but not often."

The game was played on a very personal level. The president knew all or most all the crew members he'd face. He was "sir" when he played and so was GWB. But they often

played in opposite corners. The only time rank was ever pulled was once where GW was in a game that started without him.

One of the highlights of the four years for Bush Sr. was the wedding of his daughter Dorothy "Doro" to Bobby Koch, a contractor. It was the only wedding at the base in 70 years!

Bush Senior's illustrious career positions leading up to being elected 41st President of the United States included Congressman, Ambassador to the United Nations, Director of the CIA, and 41st Vice President of the United States. Bush Senior loved to teach Washingtonians

to swim with the big fish, and his diplomatic work meant that there were a number of social events to entertain literally hundreds of foreign leaders. Among the leaders he and Mrs. Bush welcomed to Camp David were British Prime Minister Margaret Thatcher, President of Soviet Union Mikhail Gorbachev, Austra-

lian Prime Minister Robert Hawke, German Chancellor Helmut Kohl, Britain Prime Minister Sir John Major, President Carlos Salinas de Gortari of Mexico, Russian President Boris Yeltsin.

Now in his 80s and, up until recently, still physically active, President Bush Sr. celebrated his 80th and 85th birthdays with parachute jumps and told bystanders "just because you're an old guy you don't have to sit around trolling in the corner. Get out and do something," he continued "Get out and do something. Get out and enjoy life."

by John "Jack" Behrens

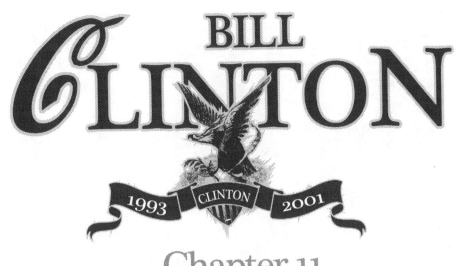

BILL CLINTON

1993 CLINTON 2001

Chapter 11
His Allergies Made Camp David Less Appealing

Bill Clinton made a momentous decision about his career after a visit to the White House Rose Garden while he was a teenager in Arkansas. Boys' Nation took him to the White House, and an informal handshaking meeting with President John F. Kennedy impressed him deeply.

Before the visit with Kennedy, Bill Clinton was a well-recognized high school saxophone player with the dream of one day playing at the White House instead of just visiting. The life of a professional musician was seductive. It wasn't going to be easy, but he was one of the best players in the state and he enjoyed music (and still does). Opinions vary on whether he made the right decision, but the truth is, he didn't give up either gig. As we all know, he continued in government and became U.S. President. What you may not know is that he continues playing the sax today and even takes his "ax" to the White House to play an occasional gig. In 1992, Clinton, played the Arsenio Hall television show and

played the blues with the house band and drew positive and negative reviews. "You know he's not that good," said one listener while another told the network news that he showed some talent.

Two piano playing presidents, Harry Truman and Richard Nixon, also displayed their talent with the 88's not far from the Rose Garden.

How many movies the Clintons saw at Camp David is unknown but we know that as he departed the White House, President Clinton said the best perk for the position was "not Air Force One or Camp David or anything else. It's the movie theater I get here because people send me these movies

all the time." The president told Stephanie Zacharek, a critic, that he did enjoy "Fight Club" and " American Beauty" which had some "insightful things to say."

While in the White House and at Camp David, the Clinton family would watch movies. The president's favorite? An old Western from 1952 which was considered one of the best produced... "High Noon" with Gary Cooper. He also enjoyed "Schindler's List". Wrote one observer; "Clinton's taste ranged from the earnest to the complex, simple and earthy, like the Naked Gun movies." He entertained Democratic governors like Gov. Anne Richards of Texas and Gov. Mario Cuomo of New York in 1993 in the viewing room.

When Clinton vaulted from governor of Arkansas to the presidency, he became the youngest U.S. President at 46 since John F. Kennedy and the third-youngest president in the country's history. Nothing new because he had been the youngest governor of Arkansas, too. While he was a moderate Democrat, he was seen as an ambitious politician who was launching a national political career in the 1980's. He entered the presidential campaign opposed to the war in Vietnam in 1992 but was attacked by veteran groups and women. He was criticized on this issue during most of his career and his two presidential terms. His opposition to the Vietnam War fueled animosity because he used a number of legitimate deferments to avoid

military service while Selective Service was inducting men of his age to serve, and the casualty death rate was growing. A Rhodes Scholar, he was in England for a period of his eligible service time.

To many males in his age bracket, however, he was a "draft dodger," and it further inflamed Americans when he was accused by a number of women of sexual misconduct. A sordid affair with a 22-year old assistant, Monica Lewinsky in the oval office brought impeachment charges in 1995-97. He denied under oath the allegations at first, but seven months later he admitted to inappropriate conduct. The House of

Representatives voted to impeach him on Dec. 9, 1998. The charge was perjury. Two-thirds of House members voted to remove him from office. The Senate, however, voted 50-50 on the obstruction charge, acquitting the president.

Allegations of misconduct came when he and his wife, Hillary, were found to be involved in a questionable real estate deal called "Whitewater." While charges of fraud and conspiracy were filed against political friends and a number went to jail, the Clintons were never indicted for criminal wrongdoing.

Social issues dominated the Clinton Administration early because he had pledged during the campaign to allow homosexuals to serve openly in the military which placed him in controversy with some staff officers and retirees. After the election, he was forced to compromise and accept a position that became known as the "don't ask, don't tell" policy.

A command military decision in foreign affairs was a failure in Clinton's first months. In 1993, he tried to capture a local warlord in Mogadishu, Somalia, by sending US Special Forces troops in a questionable raid. The mission failed and a dead American raider was shown being dragged through the streets. The operation led to a movie called "Blackhawk Down" that offered a view of heroic U.S. Rangers on an impossible mission behind enemy lines in Somalia that inferred ineptness in U.S. leadership. An Army helicopter had been shot down and the Rangers had no specific way to deal with recovery of dead or wounded. The mission collapsed and, although a very experienced American force, the Rangers were surprised by the firepower displayed by the enemy. American soldiers were forced to back off without rescuing those in the downed aircraft, as well as the rescuers. The Rangers regrouped at their base in country but realized

that the only tanks in the area were Pakistani, and the Pakistanis were reluctant to use their American made M-48 tanks to lead the rescue unit. Said letter writer Walter E. Beverly III of Rome, NY, to the Utica Observer-Dispatch on Memorial Day weekend, 2012: "In 1993...President Bush originally sent in the Marines who did a good job in making the enemy know who the boss was. If a Somali even looked like he was going to point a gun at a Marine, the Somali was shot dead, no further discussion. Then came the Clinton Administration, which pulled the Marines out and put in

the Army Rangers, Delta and a few SEALS. During the Battle of Mogadishu, 18 American men gave their lives to try to bring peace and stability to the country. More than 70 were wounded. After the battle, the military wanted to go back in and do it right. The generals wanted to send in tanks and the proper forces to do the job. The enemy was ready to capitulate. Many of the warlords wanted to give up (Mohamed) Aidid, who was the bad boy in town. Clinton lost his nerve and pulled our forces out... All our dead and wounded will have died for nothing thanks to another cowardly administration."

In his own words, Bill Clinton explained the year 1994 "as one of the hardest of my life. It began with personal heartbreak and ended in political disaster." A Republican Congress battled for the

first time over health care reform, a subject that split both parties about government interference in a matter Republicans felt was personal choice. The Clinton health plan was managed by his wife, Hillary, and along with welfare and crime prevention, they all were Democratic platform planks. The proposals failed, but in their wake, the president crafted successful legislation with Congress to introduce the North American Free Trade Agreement (NAFTA) and a General Agreement on Tariffs and Trade (GATT).

The Clintons' use of Camp David was less than his predecessors' in part because of his allergies to the plants and pollen in the heavily-wooded environment, and his interest in the day-to-day politics of Washington which frequently involved him. Yet, when he took office, he used the Camp the very first weekend. The president invited his entire cabinet to the sprawling retreat in Maryland.

Cabinet members played Eisenhower's one-hole-in-three Tees golf course, strolled the trails, swam in the Camp David pools and spent time together. To get there, the cabinet boarded a bus at 7 A.M., while the president jogged first and then took a Marine helicopter to the retreat. The meeting was ended so that cabinet members could get home to watch the Buffalo Bill-Dallas Cowboy Super Bowl XXVII game on Sunday.

Israeli Prime Minister Ehud Barak and Palestinian leader Yasser Arafat came together at the mountaintop in July, 2000. Once again, a decision couldn't be reached nor did the intensive talks put an end to a decade of conflict. Presi-

dent Clinton spent more than seven years, made 200 some telephone calls and six visits to the Middle East prior to the Camp David summit to bring peace to the troubled region, but the protagonists walked away unable to find a solution. "I've been studying," Clinton smiled in an interview with Time Magazine, "give me a test on some piece of land anywhere in Jerusalem or throughout Israel-I know the answer." Both sides agreed, however, that the U.S. was a vital partner in the quest for peace. Camp

David, meanwhile, was not a priority for Mr. Clinton during his first term in the White House. During his first year, he visited the retreat only three times in ten months. His first overnight was Thanksgiving holiday.

The Clinton summit at the Camp the next year was threatened by the feeling among observers that he had lost his opportunity to be a peacemaker. However, most observers felt the president was right in trying to resolve the issue, although he shouldn't have waited

until the end of his term to hold the summit. A later generation praised his efforts. A September 22, 2010, poll conducted by NBC and the Wall Street Journal, reported that Clinton was more popular than President Barack Obama. He had a 55 percent approval rating to Obama's 46 percent.

The Clintons continually complained about the phone system and the computers at the White House and Camp David. "He (Clinton) groused about it a lot. He likes to shake hands. He seems to like nothing better than to jump out of a limo and start shaking hands. He listens hard to people and likes to relate to them. He picks up information that way. The phone system was symbolic of the isolation, of the disconnect, of the president's inability to be connected with the public," John Podesta, aide to the President, said. The president was finally able to make changes in the Reagan and Bush systems of dialing an operator; they did away with the old way of picking up the phone and being connected to the operator. Bill Clinton brought direct dialing to the White House. He said he was concerned about his privacy.

While a debate continued among computer publications about which system was the best, Clinton staffers continued to make minor adjustments at 1600 Pennsylvania Ave. The rage at the time was Apple, a company with probably the most sophisticated and costly hardware available. Changes, some believe, were inevitable. But, White House equipment was primarily older and slower.

The Israeli and Palestinian issue continued to thwart a Middle East peace which most leaders of the time felt important to address. President Clinton, mindful of the effort of fellow Democrat Jimmy Carter to bring peace in 1978, continued to urge change in

computer hardware. But, the alterations brought more obstacles than harmony. Worse, the White House staff at the time was experienced people with little knowledge of MacIntosh, a system that took advanced knowledge and know how. You can guess the results in inter-office communication.

Most administrations have complained about internal communications in the White House. Clinton people were formerly Apple computer users, a high end system.

So, nothing at the place met their expectations. While Computer Shopper said that Macintosh computers are not as easy to use or as user-friendly as IBM compatible machines, Consumer Reports said, however, that the Mac was easier to learn. Meanwhile, administrations came and went and continued to upgrade existing White House computers. Bush and Reagan liked the idea of being able to pick up the phone in the Oval Office and in the residence and having a secretary place a call. Clinton, however, was concerned about privacy and he liked to

dial numbers himself without an operator. It was a simple matter of getting a dial tone instead of an operation. Clinton continued to complain.

W. David Watkins, assistant to the president for administration, got the job held by Ronnie Newman in the Bush administration. John Rogers had the position in the Reagan administration. He started an ad agency in 1975, before his White House stint, and in 1982 he started a long distance telephone company and later sold Hillary a 2.5 % interest in his cellular phone company.

He became deputy campaign manager for the Clinton campaign and chief financial officer. His background lacked management skills, however. He became involved in a travel budget mess, and his arrogance and lack of judgment on a number of things created chaos. He recommended dismissing all seven members of the White House travel office. It was felt Watkins had little interest in finding out what the office did. When agreeing to let the White House chef be interviewed, he said the chief steward of the White House mess should be contacted. In fact, the White House mess is a separate operation in the residence. He did the same with the travel office audit he called for. An aide told him about a seminar he attended run by KPMG Peat Marwick, and selected the firm to do the audit. What the firm found was "abysmal management" and lack of documentation for $18,000 in checks made out "cash."

Kessler interviewed White House staff and Secret Service agents and discovered what the public guessed about the relations between the two. "They argue a lot. There seems to be some kind of tension between them. There is uneasiness," one agent said. Another described Hillary in the early days as a woman who wore her hair down and no makeup around the house and sunglasses which brought agents to call her "Woodstock." At the same time, most agents agreed that she was bright. "She is intelligent, very quick. She does share in a lot of Bill's decisions," some said. There was no comparison between Hillary and Nancy Reagan. Agents thought that Nancy could be manipulative, but Hillary wasn't like that.

Agents never forgot that after Bill Clinton was sworn in, he turned to kiss his wife but, she turned away. Agents said their arguments were frequently about policy, as well as marital matters. Said a former assistant usher at the White House "I have heard from people there that they scream at each other. They can hear it down on the first floor." Hillary, one agent said, didn't throw a lamp at Bill as was widely reported, but she did throw a briefing book at him...and missed. Two Secret Service agents were driving the couple in Arkansas, and she threw the book and hit the driver. "She was hot (angry) before she got in the limousine." Agents guarding the couple know that, before he was elected, he would meet alone with pretty young women in his hotel rooms late at night. None of the agents ever reported seeing them having sex. Her power? "She is the real power," a Secret Service agent said. "She is very systematic in her thinking and very influential. The president consults her on everything."

Bill would blow up in a split second over minor things said agents and friends. For example, within five days in August, 1993, Clinton blew up at staffers in full view of reporters when he arrived in St. Louis and realized somebody had left his brief case behind. His face reddened as he yelled at the trip director, Wendy Smith, in Vail, CO. His tantrums were frequent on campaigns. "When he gets stressed out and something goes wrong, he could have a temper fit. Whoever was standing the closest caught the brunt of it."

He was in some strange company during his first term when he, Warren Harding, JFK and FDR were among the presidents who took little official time for days off. Clinton took a total 152 days off during his presidency and a sub-total of 19 days during his first year.

He was a runner but not necessarily a strong sports advocate although he and Hillary spent time cross-country skiing in the area surrounding Camp David. The president told one newspaper about a 1994 trip to Camp David: "I didn't set any Nordic records yesterday cross-country skiing but we had a wonderful time." He was known to gain weight off and on during his White House years but he didn't have the difficulties President William Howard Taft encountered. The 27th President suffered from so much girth that he had to have his security people put the ball on the tee for him when he played golf. Taft's actual weight was a closely guarded secret, but he was estimated to weigh between 300 and 350 pounds during his White House days.

While he loves chicken enchiladas, bananas, apples and vegetable beef soup he knows he has to watch his weight. Said one staffer who had watched the Clinton waist line rise and fall, "time of year plays a part, who owes who when it comes to attending some parties and not others and the political gain in attending one party over others are definitely deciders. It's what keeps Washington in motion."

What was a typical Clinton meal when they entered the White House? Broiled chicken breasts, steamed fresh veggies, rice, green salad and iced tea. Dessert was usually fruit based-a sorbet or apple crisp.

Clinton did convince Congress of the need for a North American Free Trade Agreement (NAFTA) among the US, Mexico and Canada which passed in December, 1993. It was feared it would result in thousands of jobs going to Mexico, and although that didn't happen, job losses were felt in the US. At the same time, every year of Clinton's eight years in office the crime rate fell, and when he left the White House, the rate had dropped to a 26-year low. The U.S. economy had the largest budget deficit in its history when Clinton took office. By the time he left the presidency, the country had a budget surplus of $127 billion.

His opponents insisted that Clinton couldn't take total credit for America's economic success in the early days of the 21st Century. They said he shared some blame for the financial crisis of 2007, and they laid the failure of the universal health care plan on his administration.

Yet, the scandals of his administration which began with a sexual harassment lawsuit filed by Paula Jones, followed by several other women publicly complaining about similar incidents, eroded his credibility with the public.

His administration had political successes, but it conceded it left work to be done. Mark Knoller, a longtime CBS staffer, tallied presidential visits and reported that Clinton actually spent only 152 days at Camp David. A former Clinton staff member said that the president was actually a workaholic and pointed out it would "kill him" to take a week off.

At Camp David Clinton's sexual interests spilled when a Marine guard reported on a Washington, DC, radio station that "tons of pornography" was available within the retreat. A night later, a promotion team from a Maryland night club near Camp David told radio listeners that a presidential guard had been disciplined for talking about the stash of "nudie" magazines at the retreat.

"The question was asked, the individual showed some honor and integrity and raised his hand and admitted his mistake," Major David Anderson explained. "Camp David is a premier post for our Corps. Marines are screened and selected using stringent guidelines." The White House adamantly refused to say whether the Marine's account of the magazines found at Camp David was accurate.

While Clinton listened to some advice before he entered the presidency, he obviously was most interested in golf tips from those he respected. During his teen years he had been a golfer. The Arkansan, it was reported, tried to jog every day and golf when he could. According to the "Illustrated History of White House Golf" by Shepherd Campbell and Peter Mandau, the president's golf game was described as "clouded by the matter of mulligans which President Clinton uses freely and admits to one mulligan per round and more sometimes. "A mulligan is doing a shot over without penalty. Clinton credits his strength as a golfer to being a good observer. "It's mostly because I've gotten to play with better golfers." When asked about his handicap he replied "Twelve, thirteen - something like that."

And others have to admit his golf game did improve over time. In Little Rock, AR, it is said by friends the standard arrangement was for an extra tee shot and two extra fairway strokes per nine holes when playing with the Commander-in-Chief. But observers believe the president has a good short game.

Chelsea Clinton, according to biographer, Richard Reeves, created a curious link between Ronald Reagan and the Clintons in 1985. Chelsea, then 5, wrote President Reagan a letter asking him not to go to the infamous German cemetery near Bitburg where a number of Nazi leaders and others were buried. She had seen the inspiring Rodgers and Hammerstein movie "The Sound of Music" and felt a need to write to the president: "The Nazis don't like nice people. Please don't go to the cemetery." Some aides claim they doubt Reagan ever saw the letter. As a former aide to a congressman, I would agree. Even several decades ago, letters didn't always get to the elected official, and emails had even less chance of being seen or read.

It was probably President Reagan who gave the Democratic president some simple, but overlooked information about han-

dling the details of the presidency. Just weeks after he had beaten George H.W. Bush, the two men attended a White House dinner, and Clinton paid a courtesy visit on the Reagans. They talked about soft subjects, the economy, and education, and Clinton asked Reagan for helpful suggestions. Reagan told him not to overlook the curative power of Camp David. He also

Reagan told him not to overlook the curative power of Camp David. He also told the new president that he had seen him returning salutes to military personnel, and he found them lacking. Reagan, the great communicator, told the novice new Commander-in-Chief of the American military that he needed to show more firmness and strength and a more commanding way.

told the new president that he had seen him returning salutes to military personnel, and he found them lacking. Reagan, the great communicator, told the novice new Commander-in-Chief of the American military that he needed to show more firmness and

strength and a more commanding way. Reagan had served in World War II, but he remembered why being in command was important when dealing with military units. Perception is most important, Reagan told Clinton.

The former president, an old cavalry officer, explained the hand had to come up from the side slowly and be brought down swiftly and firmly. Bystanders who passed the Oval Office remember Clinton and Reagan practicing salutes during their more than 70-minute visit. And Reagan got his reward, too. A jar of jelly beans from the 42nd president.

While both Clintons had been hurt by the sexual accusations and the scandals, both continue to lead active lives after the White House. They bought a residence in New York State where Hillary was elected US Senator, and Bill became a popular after dinner speaker for thousands of dollars a gig. But, the impeachment trial in the Senate, while unsuccessful, was only the second in the country's history. The first president to be impeached was Andrew Johnson in 1868.

Clinton added insult to injury for followers and opponents when, in the remaining days of his presidency, he issued a sweeping order to pardon 140 offenders including Hillary's brother who was freed of his lobbying fees. The President made good on his promise to help his friends. The affable Clinton smiled when he rescinded one of the two bans President George Bush made during his years. Clinton accepted the ban on smoking but quietly lifted the ban on broccoli. Clinton told close friends that Bush is a lot smarter than his image or his mannerisms indicate.

So much for healthy eating!

by John "Jack" Behrens

THE COZY MUSEUM RESTAURANT AND INN

Chapter 12
Jerry Freeze Starts Museum

Jerry Freeze and his family had much to do with the Camp David story that began in the Catoctin Mountain Park and its foothills. A long-time resident, businessman and promoter of area business, Jerry worked with military officials, civil authorities and the State of Maryland to build a combination motel, inn and museum so that those who took the time to stop in Thurmont would go away with a good feeling about what was accomplished there over 70 some years. A secrecy code caused by World War II and secret bases close by made it nearly an impossible dream. Such is the story of Thurmont, MD, Camp David and the Cozy.

This tiny country village has played host to European royalty, world leaders, the American media and dignitaries from every part of the world as the President of the United States welcomes visitors on behalf of his country. The family Freeze had already col-

lected artifacts from the WPA (Works Progress Administration) time in Maryland, as well as Herbert Hoover's days in a difficult Depression White House. Camp David was built with taxpayer money administered by the Works Progress Administration (WPA) and the Civilian Conservation Corps (CCC). Today, the camp is managed by the US Navy and the Central Intelligence Agency. The Cozy, by contrast, is the oldest operating restaurant in the state and it continues to be managed by the people who founded it, the Freeze family.

Over seven decades, a unique variety of presidential artifacts was collected by the Freeze family and others which form the historical timeline for the Cozy museum. A number of autographed photos give it authenticity, but other bits and pieces of US history crowd the museum. For example, the family decided to make sure that sitting and sleeping in the "replica beds and chairs of the famous" is possible, too. The Roosevelt room has a king-sized bed and wall hangings purchased from the Roosevelt museum in Hyde Park, NY. FDR visited the Cozy in the 1940's along with his wartime ally Winston Churchill. To celebrate their friends from England, the Freeze family added several cottages which can accommodate six. The guest houses are called the Churchill Cottages.

Gert Behrens

The Johnson Room describes the man, his personality and his need to be bigger than life and others, all at the same time. The room fits his character in tone and his 6'4" physical stature. So the Cozy has an oversized loveseat and ottoman to match Johnson's size. "You can rest easy; the king-sized spindle bed is a close facsimile to LBJ's bed at the ranch," the Freeze family spokesman said. Mrs. Johnson initiated a beautification project which generated photos and prints matching her favorite colors in wall flowers and other decorative furniture. The room lends itself to a Western look which the Freeze family attempted to convey for the Johnson Room.

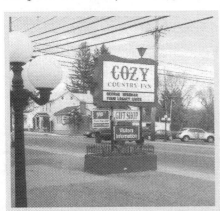

"Earlier presidents, with the possible exception of John Kennedy, Gerry Ford and even Lyndon Johnson, saw the camp as a great place to go to get away from crowds and the press," said a Freeze family spokesman.

The Carter Room follows a Southern style, yet it has a distinctive Georgian tone. The king-sized bed in the Carter Room is brass, and the pine furniture offers a homey feeling. Many of the items in the room depict Carter's love of fishing and hunting. His favorite color blue is everywhere. The room has the distinction of being used in 1978 to broadcast the summit programs. President Carter and Israeli Prime Minister Menachem Begin and Egyptian President Anwar Sadat, held the peace conference at Camp David. Famous reporters of the era Helen Thomas, David Brinkley, Walter Cronkite, Sam Donaldson and  Barbara Walters dined at the Cozy during the summits and other events held at the restaurant.

The Nixon Room features artifacts from the Richard Nixon Library. President Nixon's daughter, Julie Eisenhower, dined at the Cozy with her husband, David, as well as, Nixon law advisers John Mitchell and William Rogers. During the Nixon and Brezhnev Summit, the Cozy was the home of the Russian protocol personnel and the worldwide news agencies covering the event. The room features a queen-sized bed.

The Eisenhower Room is a charming, spacious room decorated in Mamie's favorite colors, green and pink. The ceilings and wood trim simulate the stars that were used in the light canopies at the Eisenhower farm. The pink tufted queen-sized headboard, such as Mamie had, decorates the bedroom. Knick-knacks and wall hangings depicting various parts of the Eisenhower story tastefully tell the family story. Mamie, David and Julie all dined at the Inn.

The Kennedy Room has a huge canopy over a king-sized bed reflecting the style of the bed JFK used while he was in the White House. There is a replica of the famous Kennedy rocker, too. The furniture in the room fits Mrs. Kennedy's tastes. Some of the Kennedy cabinet had visited the Cozy over the years since his death.

Not far away, the Reagan Cottage offers a different view of White House life. This romantic cabin features a queen-size water bed and a corner mirrored Jacuzzi. The unit was left as it was the day CBS network, "Face the Nation", interviewed Reagan while he was running for his second term in 1984. Leslie Stahl was the young interviewer at the camp "where the presidential family can actually be a family," said Anna Perez, former First Lady Barbara Bush's press secretary. "Do you know what a luxury it is for the president?", said George Stephanopoulos, Clinton's Senior Policy Advisor on Policy and Strategy, who was one of members who stayed in the Clinton suite.

The cost of operating the office has increased substantially today. Access to Camp David is limited to crew, said Lt. Gen. Richard G. Trefry, former military assistant to President Bush. "Camp David is restricted to crew members, support personnel and Presidential guests," he said. The camp is under the operational control of the White House Military Office. The operational control is handled by a staff of Navy officers who are hand-picked from Naval ranks. It has been that way since sailors were told that the USS Potomac would be beached at the outbreak of World War II and they could transfer to other Navy vessels or serve in land units. You are selected to serve at Camp David, I was told a number of times.

News agencies, such as the Associated Press, United Press, NBC, CBS, CNN, ABC, MPT, United Press International, Reuters, MPT, AFP and the White House Press Corps, also have rooms in the Cozy.

A personal invitation from the president is the only way to get past US Marine security at the compound gate. You'll probably still face scrutiny. Media are not allowed unless specifically invited.

Accountants say budgeting such an operation is very difficult. The estimate by those who are experienced in making such a call believe that Camp David costs are over one hundred million a year and rising.

Jerry Freeze

Even those who weren't excited about the place thought it was nonetheless a beautiful spot. President Carter said so, and so did President Barack Obama. Carter described it as truly beautiful with cottages all named after trees and paths snaked down one side of the mountain. The cottages are sheltered by a dense growth of stately oak, poplar, ash, locust, hickory, and maple trees. A security fence surrounds about 125 acres of the rocky terrain, and living quarters close by add to the comfort proximity of being in the woods. The living quarters offer a feeling of isolation and informality. A few golf carts and bikes are available, but most people choose to walk among the cottages, we are told. One side of the camp fence was built during the Roosevelt years.

In the good 'old days when W.R. "Willy" Freeze was busy creating the Cozy, he had help from a variety of sources. Mamie Eisenhower showed up to visit with Mary Freeze, H.Q. Miller, who in the 1940s, drew dramatic illustrations for the well-known comic strip, The Shadow and The Cozy, and family member Becky Freeze, who produced The Cozy newspaper edition. Charles Colley, an artist and historian, created a 24-foot mural of  the Cozy Village of Shoppes. The 78th edition carried the mural. Those were the days! 1940s.

A small clearing of 8 acres was cut outside the security fence in the latter part of the Roosevelt years. The crew used it for a softball diamond in 1955. During the Eisenhower years, it was enlarged and a hangar and a skeet range were added, which became a popular pastime, it seems.

Celebrating the Christmas holiday began in the 1950s, Jerry told me when we talked in the 1970's. "The enthusiastic remarks from our customers about the holiday decorations caused me to return every year. We have a tree decorated for the troops, and we have another inside the caboose, that features homemade decorations brought in by our customers. Cozy is aglow with Christmas cheer at the holiday," Jerry says.

The first figurine at the Cozy? A jolly Santa Claus.

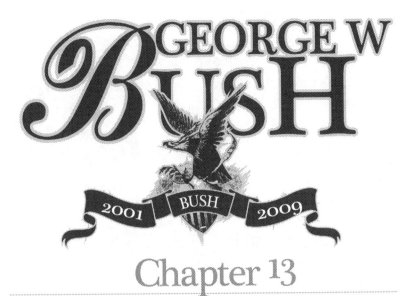

Chapter 13
Father, Son Differences Created Difficulties

George W. Bush had the difficulty many young men have in life try-ing to follow the footsteps of a successful father. While he had his epi-sodes and escapades, he also demonstrated over time contriteness and commitment to the family. It wasn't always conveyed by spoken words because he was uncomfortable in front of audiences. But it was his re-sponses to problems that mattered. They were sincere, some said.

He had help, of course. Mom and dad were certainly cheer-leading along with other family members, too. But so was a very loyal and strong wife, Laura, who stood by him when together-ness was vital. Family does make a difference and the Bush family was no exception. Without a doubt, the family and the nation were severely tested during his eight years as Commander in Chief.

George and Laura Welch had a three month courtship after they met at a backyard barbecue in 1977. He proposed and they married Nov. 5 of the same year. The couple settled in Midland, TX. George left his family's Episcopal Church to join Laura's United Methodist Church. The couple has twin daughters Jenna and Barbara.

Before his marriage, Bush had a number of alcohol experiences and the result was the suspension of his driving license and a fine of $150. His alleged use of drugs involved military enlisted claiming he was seen taking them at Camp David. Such charges were never fully supported.

His wife, he says, gave him back his life. "I saw an elegant beautiful woman who turned out not only to be elegant and beautiful but very smart and willing to put up with my rough edges and I must confess she smoothed them off over time" he told others. His hobbies include golf and smoking cigars, which isn't politically correct, but many of his supporters say make him a man's man.

Bush moved his family to Washington D.C. in 1988 to work on his father's bid for the presidency. He trailed John McCain in the New Hampshire primary and lost that primary to McCain. But in the campaign he scored a number of surprises before the Texas

governor traveled cross country to try to lock up a victory. On November 7 he had 29 states plus Florida to win the 2000 presidency. He returned to win again in 2004.

To his credit, a controversial bill "No Child Left Behind" which even got the support of Democratic Sen. Ted Kennedy of MA was signed into law in 2002. Although it passed, the measure has received mixed reviews.

Meanwhile at Camp David, George became virtually a weekly regular. He visited more than his father and Ronald Reagan who set a record until Jimmy Carter and Richard Nixon both spent time using the retreat to hide from the media.

While most observers and Mark Knoller, a CBS Radio White House Correspondent who is considered the unofficial record keeper on president's visits, believes Bush may hold the record for total number of visits, although another author discovered that

FDR probably holds the record. "Franklin Roosevelt was president for 12 years and nobody's going to beat his record because he was just in office longer than anybody else."

His presidency faced the same struggle as Franklin Delano Roosevelt's Administration had in 1941. Americans were attacked on their homeland in an unprovoked act of war on a beautiful Tuesday morning, Sept. 11, 2001, when the World Trade Center in New York City, the Pentagon and a thwarted attempt to damage the White House and Capitol took the lives of nearly 3,000 people. The difference was that American lives and property were at stake not Filipinos and Philippine property. In hours, it escalated Bush's presidential duties and made him a wartime president, although the United States Congress hadn't declared war. Yet, he didn't escape criticism even when most Americans felt he was doing a "good" job leading the country.

A controversial decision to seek an appointment with the Texas Air National Guard a few years before the attack made it appear that he sought exemption from the Vietnam War. He never served in the war although he continued in the guard and learned to fly jet fighters. Those things bothered Texans and many others across the country.

His father, George H.W. Bush, told the world that his son "faced the greatest challenge of any president since Abraham Lincoln." No one disagreed. The attack was the work of radicalized Middle Eastern dissidents who had infiltrated the country and sought to kill Americans and destroy infrastructure. Their purpose appeared to be death and destruction and, although their goals would have been more devastating had all their efforts been fulfilled, a resilient America withstood the assault. Frightened and alarmed citizens responded quickly to brutal television images even more vivid than Pearl Harbor which was covered by radio and news-

reel cameras. Americans saw powerful footage of the horror of large jets plowing into the Twin buildings that made the Big Apple so famous, the vaunted Pentagon and Pennsylvania countryside destroyed. The carnage was everywhere only this wasn't from a field of battle; it was innocent citizens traveling for business, family and personal reasons. It was an assault on American values, people and lifestyle; the most powerful of the twenty-first century. It happened when America's own innovations - wide-bodied jets and technology were turned against itself.

A poignant example of how the younger George demonstrated the way family and duty influenced him came shortly after he left the White House and retired to his Texas ranch. Although continually hammered and criti-

cized by the Obama Administration for creating huge problems in America financially and morally, Bush became silent. Aides tried to counter the lack of a Republican voice and little to no White House response to the Democrat attacks. But the lack of balance caused the public to swing to Independent and Democrat voices. However, the president's compassion came in less demonstrative ways. The Bushes, for example, showed up at the Dallas-

Fort Worth TX Airport in support of a group of local women welcoming home soldiers and their families. The organizer of the welcoming committee said she was "amazed to see the Bushes quietly waiting with others to shake hands and wish the soldiers well." The warm greetings exchanged told how

important the gathering was for the welcomers and those being greeted. George was in a blue T-shirt and dark pants and Laura wore a pants suit. The pictures taken were testimony to the value of the event. As every newspaper person knows, "a photo is worth a 1,000 words."

One historian called George Bush's presidency the most stressful of any modern day leader. Several years before, American security was tested again when about 100 FBI agents fanned

out in a wooded area several miles from an ex-army scientist's apartment when he became a person of interest after a report of anthrax spores. Five people died and 18 were infected in October, 2001 when letters containing the deadly spores were received by media and government offices in Washington. The fact that the person's apartment was so close to the presidential Camp David retreat raised speculation. The FBI closed off one and one/half of icy miles and took added precautions of having divers nearby for evidence of materials. In the course of the investigation, a Frederick, MD city spokesperson told media that

two scientists regularly monitor water in the area for possible contamination. Frederick is just a few miles from Camp David.

In the midst of gloomy news and more worries about tomorrow, George Bush could find time to create and pursue interest in a new kind of game at Camp David; Wallyball. The Bushes enjoyed the Westminster Teak furniture purchased for Camp David by the Naval Support facility.

George made his final visit to Camp David Jan. 16, 2009, and it had to be a visit filled with many emotions. He had the chance to see old faces among the enlisted and staff officers and there were smiles as many remember how he and his father dueled for Wallyball victories on the Camp David court. Their lanky physique gave them a competitive edge sometimes. A California game brought to Camp David in early 2000, the Bushes became outstanding players. George Sr. was considered one of the best with George W. just

a step behind. It was said that it created a great diversion for those who played it and those who watched it. It was also considered a tension reliever during stressful periods of the eight years. Said one player in the early years, there were six to seven tournaments and healthy competition in games and among teams. "Nothing has been dissed by the first family more than Camp David. Aides to Al Gore and George say they're over the chance of seeing their nameplate on a Camp David golf cart (as a winner)."

The Texas governor has a real thing for the rustic retreat having spent years in its log cabins when dad was prez. White House correspondents said they have something to cheer about with George W. now that he doesn't have round the clock weekend duty at the Camp. There are 2,200 racquetball clubs and a good number partner with Wallyball groups. The Bushes loved the game, staff members told me. Said one: "Whenever Bush played, he only wanted to play with family or crew (permanent assigned people at the camp) Tournaments were routinely held to see who had the level of skill needed for the First Family. He always picked the top four players to play against. The goal of every player I knew at Camp David was to spike it on the president! We played on a personal level. The president knew almost every crew member who played. He was 'sir' and we were known by our Christian names."

"The only time there could be a dispute," the staffer laughed was when he (GWB) was "late and somebody started the game without him!"

Camp David, Wallyball, critical command decisions during difficult times, finding the Lord on a mountaintop called Catoctin

in solitary moments when he was alone...That was George W. Bush's presidency. It didn't play out as he expected but then neither did Richard Nixon, Bill Clinton or

Barack Obama's days in the White House and Camp David.

The president's Secretary of State, Condoleeza Rice, the first black woman to hold the position, said it best on the back cover of her book "No Higher Honor", "Today's headlines and history's judgments are rarely the same. If you are too attentive to the former, you will most certainly not do the hard work of securing the latter."

by John "Jack" Behrens

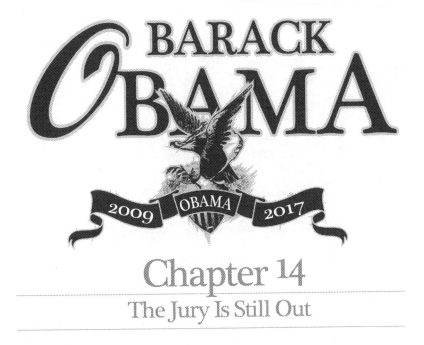

Chapter 14
The Jury Is Still Out

President Barack Obama, like his predecessors, says he loves what Camp David offers and where it is located but he and Michelle, he adds, lead very active lives and they have two busy teenaged children who have equally frenetic lives with school and outside activities. As a result, he hasn't seen as much of the president's retreat as he would like. His first overnight in recent months, for example, was last May when he met with fifty chief executives at the G8 Summit.

More than 50 heads of state have visited Camp David in the last seven decades but 2012's G8 meeting was the first time more than two foreign heads of state had gathered there at the same time, the Associated Press reported. White House aides admitted that when you host a G8 summit of eight nations and their leaders, finding accommodations for such a variety of vanities and staff is overwhelming. The G8 at the Maryland retreat in May 2012 was

the largest gathering the US had ever had at the mountain retreat in its 70 years. "Camp David has just got a special atmosphere to it," Mike Forman, one of Obama's economic advisers told reporters, adding that meetings in such a friendly location allows "the guests to enjoy a series of informal, unplanned, spontaneous meetings. That is exactly what the president had in mind." The G8 summit was originally scheduled for Chicago where Obama hosted the NATO conference but it was changed to escape the anti-Wall Street protestors and to give the president and his guests a chance to talk "in a more casual backdrop."

"Camp David has just got a special atmosphere to it," Mike Forman, one of Obama's economic advisers told reporters, adding that meetings in such a friendly location allows "the guests to enjoy a series of informal, unplanned, spontaneous meetings.

G8 SUMMIT 2012

He's likeable, he gives answers that appeal to many, he resonates with others and he uses the presidential jet "Air Force One" so often that the ground crew has a hard time keeping a maintenance schedule. Among many fathers and mothers he is a role model parent who puts his children ahead of his weekly plans. While the world wondered and awaited word on the capture of Quadhafi, the president and his family bicycled in the in Manuel F Correllus State Forest on the 109th anniversary of the first presidential motorcade. In the same week, he sang about his hometown Chicago and joined an all star cast of musicians including BB King, Booker T. Jones and Mick Jagger in a PBS Special at the White House.

President Obama, like his predecessors, is supportive of the camp and its mission, although at times, he says that his children come first. Few will argue with his stance. He and Michelle, he adds, lead very active lives and they have two busy teenaged daughters who have school activities crowding their calendars. The result is that Obama hasn't seen that much of the president's retreat, although he says he wants to.

It's rustic, some add, not necessarily luxurious, others contend suggesting it doesn't fit the style of urban Chicagoans. At Camp

David you have your own well-equipped lodge and White House chefs if you need them. Your personal one-hole fits three golf course, swimming pools including a heated one, 24-7 security, shuffleboard court, lodges for family and friends, bowling alley, basketball and tennis courts inside and out, and a movie theater in the White House and at Camp David.

The president celebrated his 52nd birthday with golf and a quick getaway to Camp David with friends. To make sure he was able to get in a game of golf on Sunday, he left the White House just after 8 a.m. No one noticed whether he was driving his golf cart or not. He showed

Americans he could lead and charm even though the G-8 Summit didn't alter much or many opinions. Of course in a world that changes colors more often than a bandstand at a rock concert, anything can happen in the next 24 hours. Most believe the G-8 was a

suc-

For example, the camp was virtually opened for visitors to see and media were given more access than usual during the G-8 meeting. It wasn't advertised but the amount of coverage and the number of visitors was larger than previous events. Yet, the administration was careful to stay within the secrecy code that has continued for 70 years!

cessful gathering and one of the reasons, many say, was the atmosphere and intimacy created by the Maryland mountain retreat itself. In other words, many believe he knows how to use what is available and gain the advantages it offers. For ex-

ample, the camp was virtually opened for visitors to see and media were given more access than usual during the G-8 meeting. It wasn't advertised but the amount of coverage and the number of visitors was larger than previous events. Yet, the administration was careful to stay within the secrecy code that has continued for 70 years!

Camp David creates its own ambience. The perks are tempting to the hosts as well as the guests. You have your own well-equipped lodge,

White House chefs for special affairs, your personal one hole fits all golf course, swimming pools including a heated one, the best 24-7 security our nation can provide, shuffleboard court, lodges for family and friends, a bowling alley, basketball court, tennis courts inside and out, a theater and a projectionist to show movies at any time of the day or night, a skeet range and four pool tables. Of course, you can play solitaire if

One of the interesting stories about Camp David under Obama's watch is the quiet transformation of Evergreen Chapel, the nondenominational chapel built during the Bushes' tenure. Chaplain Carey Cash, nephew of famed singer Johnny Cash, has helped Obama settle the issue of home church by following the lead of George W. Bush and declaring Evergreen to be the family's church during their residency.

you want. The movies include nostalgic oldies as well as top Hollywood hits.

One of the interesting stories about Camp David under Obama's watch is the quiet transformation of Evergreen Chapel, the nondenominational chapel built during the Bushes' tenure. Chaplain Carey Cash, nephew of famed singer Johnny Cash, has helped Obama settle the issue of home church by following the lead

of George W. Bush and declaring Evergreen to be the family's church during their residency. Commander Cash is a perfect fit for the base, the president and the military and he has lived up to his reputation. Cash's father Roy was a fighter pilot for 30 years and Carey's sister Kellye, was Miss America in 1987. His mother, Billie, ran a Christian ministry and authored several books about faith. The commander's strong faith was nurtured at the Southwestern Baptist Theological Seminary and strengthened by good family values.

Carey was a graduate of the Citadel military academy and a former professional football player before he was assigned to Catoctin Mountain duty. According to friends and supporters, Commander Cash is a true believer and fervent about his faith. He is also said to be committed to spreading Christianity within the armed forces. He has told many of his audiences that he firmly believes a "wall of angels" will protect his comrades from danger.

Security continues to be a concern for those who protect the president. July 2, 2011, an F-15E forced a two-seater passenger plane to land at Hagerstown when it was 6 miles from the residence and out of radio communication. Since 2002, the incidents overhead have increased and caused concern.

A 2010 poll by leading presidential scholars ranks Barack

Obama as the 15th best president. In a Siena College study which surveyed 238 scholars at US colleges and universities, Obama ranked two places behind Bill Clinton who was selected 13th best and three places better than Ronald Reagan, who is ranked 18th. However, Obama's Fall 2013 poll numbers have dropped, and demonstrated that his popularity is slipping.

There are gorgeous sunrises and sunsets in the surrounding valleys (only on good days because Maryland mountains are frequently shrouded in fog). To visiting foreign leaders, there is the political allure of the place where Reagan, Nixon, Carter, Clinton, and world leaders met to talk and decide weighty issues.

He explains in his two books, Dreams of My Father, and The Audacity of Hope that his grandfather was a Muslim and that he spent two years in Indonesian Muslim school studying the Koran. In the later book, Audacity of Hope, he claims that his father raised a Muslim but by the time he was reunited with his mother he was a "confirmed atheist." The books haven't satisfied many about his views of church and state or even his birthright.

The Obama presidency is best seen in footwear. On Saturday morning of the G8, the president exchanged his dress shoes for sneakers and a visit to the Camp David Gym where he met British Prime Min-

ister David Cameron on side by side treadmills. Later, he shot some hoops as the group waited for the summit to continue.

To many Americans, however, Camp David is barely recognized. It carries the mystique that Franklin D. Roosevelt discovered when he saw it in 1942. But it has continued a secrecy code that reduces it to a footnote instead of the shrines that were expected to highlight its existence after the war.

by John "Jack" Behrens

INDEX

INDEX

Pets

Places

Presidents

by John "Jack" Behrens

ABOUT THE AUTHOR

I first started reading about Camp David in 1964-65 when I was working for the Associated Press various times Of the year from Lancaster, OH to Huntington, WVA to Ashland, KY to Utica, NY I scanned hundreds of stories about the presidents and their families to visitors to the camp, Add to that a web site that offered lots of details about the activities at Camp David called Camp David Tour Presidential Retreat and the outstanding Presidential Libraries which permitted me to put graphics to the words. It was hours of work daily for better than fourteen years broken up by illness including a near death episode that nearly finished me. But the Lord enabled me to finish it and provide you with a partial look at the cost of running a huge government.

It's a look inside at how governments run on idle. My thanks to Helen and Bill King who explained the incredible and the serious problem with letting computers run government. I am interested in your thoughts about government out of control. Write to me at jbehrens@roadrunner.com